MW00325573

NAMACRAY

Nama~~ste~~ CRAY

8 Ways to Bow to Your Inner Crazy

Katie B. Happyy

LIONCREST
PUBLISHING

COPYRIGHT © 2021 KATIE BURKE

All rights reserved.

NAMACRAY

8 Ways to Bow to Your Inner Crazy

ISBN   978-1-5445-2072-8   *Hardcover*
       978-1-5445-2071-1   *Paperback*
       978-1-5445-2070-4   *Ebook*

This book is a bow to you, to me, and to all the broken badasses out there who know there's something more.

This book is not teaching you anything new. It's about reminding you of the things that you've always known but life experiences have made you forget.

Mark up this book and come back daily to take my words and make them your own.

Life's too short to be anything other than awesome.

Cheers!

Contents

Introduction

Life has a beautiful way of giving me fucked-up happy endings, and most of them, I never even asked for. Learning how to embrace these strange gifts has been a lifetime of self-work and daily commitments to remember that it's not my job to find balance but to create it. We all have the choice to live as if everything has meaning, or as if nothing does, and I have chosen the former. Luck is the residue of my life's narrative, and that's how I choose to write it.

I didn't know that women could have happy endings. Well, happy-ending *massages*, that is. I always thought it was an international "boys only" club. I mean, it seems more obvious that an erection would be the universal sign of arousal, right? Girls are *way* too stuck in their heads, or at least, that was the narrative I was writing.

I'd just gotten back from leading a yoga retreat in Italy when two girls from NYC told me that they often got happy-ending massages in Europe. As you can imagine, I was completely shocked. *Was I just too closed off to know that was a thing? Yeah, I'm guarded, but how did I not know? I'm fucking forty-plus countries traveled, a global goddess.* I could feel my Jersey ego flaring with insecurity: I hate not knowing or feeling left out.

In all of my keynote speeches, international retreats, classes, and friendships, I always advocate for dreaming bigger. Like, Oprah-giving-out-cars-to-the-audience big. If you can't think that *maybe* it could happen for you, then there's no chance that the doors will open...and that relates to all barriers in life, even the sexual ones.

"Maybe I'm not thinking big enough," I'd told the retreaters the week before in Italy. "I've got to think Oprah big. O big—*orgasm* big," and laughed at the far-fetched notion. It has always taken a lot mentally for me to orgasm, so there's no way a random guy at a massage parlor could get me there... but fuck. The world is a weird and wonderful place, and I somehow ended up having a completely new experience at the same forty-dollar massage parlor I'd visited many times before, right under my yoga studio.

On this particular Monday night, I didn't even know who the masseuse was. Most of them barely speak English, but since there's always just been an unspoken agreement of no talking, it didn't even matter. And honestly, I liked it that way. As I relaxed into the massage, I noticed that he started off a little glute- and butt-heavy, and I could feel myself getting a little turned on. I giggled to my single self, enjoying the sensual experience a *little* too much.

As I did the normal flip from face-down to face-up on the massage table, his hands started to move a little lower than normal on my pectorals and breasts. Having led many trips to India and China, I already knew that breast massages were a normal part of an Eastern, non-sexual massage called *ambianga*. In *ambianga*, they use hot oil to move along your energy lines, traveling over your nipples, through the creases of your legs, and even into your belly button (which gets a little fingered).

"Is this okay?" he asked, and I nodded, feeling totally comfortable—and even a bit excited. It had been months since I'd been touched by anyone like this, and I was going to thoroughly enjoy whatever this was.

"Do you want to finish?" he asked.

"Sure," I replied, not knowing exactly what he meant, but secretly hoping that some magic was about to happen. As he massaged my calf muscle, he quickly moved one of his fingers over my labia lips...and within ten seconds, it was over. A *fucking happy ending*. He kept going down my legs, as if this was completely normal for him, and finished massaging the knots out of my feet before leaving the room...just like the 400 other *normal* massages that I'd had at that place.

I laid there in shock, not quite believing that this was an actual thing. Even in the first eight seconds of the ten-second rub, I had the deepest doubts that I would even orgasm. And when I did, the whole thing was treated as just another ordinary, business-as-usual.

When I walked out to pay—still shocked and blushing—I got my first look at the smaller Asian man who'd brought me to ecstasy moments earlier...and he handed me a fucking punch card! Apparently, with "Michael," the tenth one is free. *Do I tip him more?* I wondered. *No one is going to believe me. Like what?!*

Did I want a happy-ending massage? Fuck no. Did I go back later to get another one? Fuck no. Did I receive one because I was suddenly open to it after years of not knowing that it was a possibility? Who knows—that's the magic cray-cray of this world. I like to think that because those beautiful NYC retreaters opened my eyes to the possibility that women could actually orgasm in a massage, the world decided to bring it into my life, so that I could experience one as well. Weirdly, that massage was a gift that I never even asked for, but one I desperately needed—which is the very essence of "nama-cray."

"Nama" means to bow in Sanskrit. Well, my life (and probably yours, too, if you're reading this) is not always "woo-woo, namaste." I'm not always gracefully bowing to the light in other people with a gentle smile. But as a sarcastic, crass Jersey girl whose life choice was to waste her international business degree to become a master yogi, I've figured out that our twenty-first-century world is more nama-cray than namaste. Don't get me wrong, though: I'm not perfect by any means, and I definitely don't have it all figured out. In fact, some nights I give up, end it with some tequila, and try again the next day. However, one thing I do know is that the adventure life throws at all of us is worth taking. We all come into this world with an inhale, then leave it with an exhale, and every breath in between is a daily practice of discovering why we are here. My hope is that you open your mind to just a few possibilities, take at least one technique that adds value to your life, and practice it in your daily life.

But don't just believe every word that I say. This book, just like everything else ever written, is one person's perspective in a world with billions of perspectives. I'll be sorting through my personal cray-cray stories, offering timeless tools and techniques that have worked for me, and presenting my truth—the only thing I know. In my vast years of exploring both what my truth is and what it can become, I've stumbled onto some deep understandings. Look through my lens's perspective, then consider how it adds dimension to yours. Question it, use it, and personalize it in your favor.

Maybe it's time to finally honor the beautiful crazy in you, the wonderful crazy that you've always known. Use your dusty inner toolbox to take a legendary bow to all the insanity that life throws at you. Bow to your *own* story.

So now, I'm bowing to you, to me, and to all the broken badasses out there who know there's a better way to handle the Universe's unexpected hiccups. Just remember: life doesn't always give us the endings that we want, but it can surprise us all with happy endings that we've never even dreamed of.

CHAPTER 1

Bow to This Moment

My long piano fingers tightly gripped the steering wheel. I'd never seen my tan hands go white. I couldn't even recognize my own knuckles.

WTF, world? I went into urgent care thinking that I'd had an allergic reaction to my Sunday Bloody Mary and came out paralyzed. The word "palsy" kept repeating in my mind. *Fuck that doctor.* He didn't know what he was talking about. Didn't he see my beautiful smile? My giant, white, horse teeth? There's no way that half of my face couldn't work. There's no way that I, Katie B. Happyy, couldn't use the right side of my face.

"You have an 80 percent chance of recovery," he'd said crassly. I wanted to throw my cell phone at his face. When you're sick, you don't hear the C+ grade chance of healing. You hear the negative part, the part that says you have a 20 percent chance of *not* healing.

I caught a glance of my disfigured face in the sun visor mirror, tried to summon the neurotransmitters to do their normal duties, and commanded my body, "Lift right eyebrow." Only the left side lifted. "Flare right nostril." Only the left fanned out like a cow. "Close right eyelid." My right eye rolled up into its socket, but the lid didn't move. "Right side, smile." The left side moved my lips completely over, as if to pick up the dead weight of the right side. My usually brilliant smile had morphed into a sideways, half-assed one.

Holy shit. How did I not notice that the swelling was actually paralysis? I'm a goddamn yoga teacher: I'm supposed to be so in tuned and connected with my body every day. I can sense up to the second when I am going to start bleeding on my period. I can give myself an orgasm without even touching myself. I have the core awareness to stand on my fucking hands for sixty seconds in the middle of a room. I'm namaste AF, so how could I wake up paralyzed one day without noticing any changes?

I'm officially broken. My zen namaste is now officially nama-cray. Still in shock, my mind ping-pongs between fear of the word "paralyzed" and back to not believing that it's real. *Oh, Matthew. What am I going to tell my beautiful, brown-eyed*

Matthew? His smile competed with mine for both size and authenticity. His beautiful white teeth paralleled my blinding pearly whites, and together, we were an unstoppable smiling power couple. The pseudonym "Katie B. Happyy," originally given as a sarcastic nickname to a bitter Jersey transplant, felt more authentic when I was with him. I could "be happy" side by side with this gentle giant. *Fuck me. Fuck this doctor. He can't be right. I can't be paralyzed.*

Just last month, I'd had the yoga career highlight of my life. My sponsorship and partnership as a Lululemon ambassador enabled me to teach at Wanderlust in Aspen over the Fourth of July weekend. This festival is every western yoga teacher's dream: not only did I get to teach four workshops over four days, but I also had a fan club of my closest, most amazing friends come to support me. I even had a presenter badge! Me, the Jersey-born, loco, San Diego yoga teacher with a bad attitude and a ridiculous affinity towards all things tequila, had a fucking presenter badge.

I smiled like a goddamn flashlight in that upstairs yoga hall, a smile that my dad had always called his $20,000 smile. After years of retainers and headgear, at least my pearly straight whites had amounted to something.

My spunky, sassy, flamboyant buddy Tabu. This 6 percent body fat, legs-for-days dancer started as a movement mentor of mine who became a close friend. I've always been a sucker for characters, as long as they own who they are, and boy, does he own it. He's been known to hump me in push-ups, booty-drop during cardio bursts, and yell at everyone unable to "spread their legs" during crunches. We bicker about the most basic bitch stuff, like whose kick is higher or whose skin will last until old age better (his deeply-toned skin is perfect, but I never let on). As entertaining as I find him as a person, I'm only willing to participate in his shenanigans because I know that his heart is so big. He's one of the only people who challenges me with honesty, loyalty, and truth, and I was thrilled that he took time out of his vacation just to celebrate me out in Aspen.

As I kept driving home, my mind wandered deeper into the memory of our Fourth of July madness. On the actual holiday, I'd had my most nerve-racking session of all.

"This way to True North" signs lined the entirety of Snowmass Village. My dry San Diego skin loved the wet green grass that lined the area like street signs, guiding you from tent to tent. I walked five steps in front of Matthew, my amazing man of four years, with sheer glee guiding my steps at an insatiable speed. I couldn't soak it in fast enough, still in disbelief that I'd landed my big toes (literally size eleven feet) in this pro-verbial grass. *Wanderlust! Me? I am the shit! Verify and give me that blue checkmark now, Instagram!*

Typically, my bleeding heart would be disgusted by the overpriced snow gear and insane prices for kale blended up in a cup, but it felt like this Aspen Snowmass Village was snow-in-summer perfection. My gratitude completely blinded my disgust of twelve-dollar coffees and breakfast burritos.

When we first arrived, I was shuttled to the presenter tent. My hard plastic badge read "Presenter Katie B. Happyy," *and* I had a different color wristband than my friends. My god, even the smallest thing like a presenter badge made me change how I viewed myself in an instant. I felt so important, and significance was my love language.

I danced my way out of that office with an uncontained, stupid smile. Matthew, who was patiently waiting outside for me, had that knowing smile that made me blush and giggle. He's so fucking good at celebrating me. His empathy made me want to jump his bones right there on that ski mountain.

Not knowing the slightest thing about Colorado, let alone Snowmass Mountain, we used their Wanderlust Compass map to guide us everywhere.

"Babe, we should skip the morning class you planned with Sean Corne. The HillTop Venue takes twenty minutes just to travel to, so let's go up early and scope it out," Matthew said. "We can text your groupies how to get there later." He knew all too well that my directional sense would fail me on this quest up a new mountainside without proper time to prepare.

My nerves were so fired up at that point that he could have told me to start running under the Gondola toward the workshop location, and I would have said yes. I'd follow anything that six-foot-one Lebanese Italian god told me; he was always my grounding point and kept my fiery spirit rooted.

Have you ever ridden up a ski lift with just grass under your feet? It felt so weird having to take my sandals into my hands for fear of losing them to the weeds twenty feet below. Oh, but the freedom of swinging my legs as we were carried blissfully to the top of the ski lift made me feel like a kid again. The corners of my mouth were lifted so high I could barely keep the slobber from getting stuck in my hair. Matthew's right hand held my left hand with supportive delight, and I giggled as I watched his long brown dreads dance behind his back.

This can't be real, I thought. One minute, I'm a basic Inner-SteadyYoga teacher, and one phone call later, I'm riding a gondola up to teach at Wanderlust. I remember gazing down at the grass, not wanting to forget it. *Life changes so quickly. We forget so much. I personally forget so much.*

When we reached the HillTop venue, a dry erase board was set up as I'd requested. The previous class had just found a spot nestled in some tree stumps and odd rocks that looked easy to sit on. If the classroom desks were rocks and tree stumps, then the blackboard and backdrop were the surrounding mountain peaks. How was anyone going to stay present in my session with this amazing scenery? Even my interest in my own content was melting into the backdrop of the mountains, causing my inner creativity to flare.

I scratched my initial plans of using the dry erase board to help them drop limiting beliefs, deciding that we needed to move mountains with our minds. Instead of guiding them through writing exercises to shed old thought patterns, we were going to use the mountains to ease their thinking patterns. Thank you, Universe, for always providing the tools I need, even if I didn't actually want them in the first place.

As the class's start time approached, I pace-danced around Matthew, watching empty ski lift after empty ski lift dropping off the ghosts of the students I so desperately wanted to meet. *Twenty minutes, my ass;* it took us closer to thirty. *Calm down, KBeezy. They will come.*

Seven minutes into the proposed class time, my crew of American-flag-faced ladies hopped off the lift. They were smitten with the ride, the view, and the fact that their friend was getting to teach on top of a fucking mountain in Aspen. I was exploding to see them, my team, my friends, who had flown all this way to show up for me. And man, did they show up.

Time is one of my love languages, and they gave it hard. Six days, including travel, thousands of dollars on hotels, flights, and tickets, and most importantly, they cheered me on in a foreign yoga land of more experienced and better yoga teachers than I am. I sat cross-legged in half lotus, downhill from their seats on the rocks. Their view was divine.

"I am so grateful you chose to spend your afternoon here with me," I began. "I know about the time you all invested to get up here to HillTop, but I hope that by the end of our time together, you'll know that the peace you've gained during our work together was worth it. I'm Katie B. Happyy, reigning all the way from San Diego, California. Don't be fooled, though. I'm a Jersey girl who loves a sarcastic plot twist. Let's see what this hour has to teach us. You in?"

No response. I knew better.

"If you're with me, put up an imaginary cup of your favorite drink. Mine's a Cadillac margarita, Don Julio, no triple sec or agave, with tajin on the rim. Once you've done that, just hold up your imaginary cup and say CHEERS. So, you with me?"

Fifty percent said an emphatic "CHEERS," with the newbs riding the coattails of my posse.

I laughed, big and loud. Facilitation is my life-long master class. My brain gets a tiny tickle orgasm anytime I see a facilitator hold space like a boss. It's a beautiful recipe of giving them just enough to like you, a dab to be jealous of you, a teaspoon to laugh about with you, and a pinch of sarcasm.

Masters at the craft can make anyone feel like they're the only ones being spoken to, and yet, somehow simultaneously supported by the entirety of their peers there.

There's a beautiful dance I take part in every time I step into one of my yoga classes; this dance is what has kept me interested in teaching yoga for four years, full time, and twenty-plus classes a week. Every class is new, and every hour is an opportunity to co-create the current world with my students. What does the yoga class have to teach me? What can the moment bring that I can't even see yet? Being what I qualified as a fucking master in my power yoga field, I got off on changing it all on the fly, based on the energy. It kept me on my toes. *Life changes all the time, so why shouldn't your flow in a sixty-minute yoga class change, too?*

I decided to start this sky-high workshop with movement. "Everyone, leave your journals and pens on the ground. I believe that before we can do the work inward, we have to work out. Let's raise the vibration of this mountaintop.

"I was raised to be an awkward dancer, and I never felt quite right in my skin dancing. Cheers if you're with me on that!" A couple of awkward cheers sprang out from the crowd.

I smiled, then said, "There's a song by Walk the Moon that says, 'Don't you dare look back, just keep your eyes on me; I said you're holding back, she said shut up and dance with me.'

It reminds me that the past is the past. All we have is right now to shut up our heads, our worries, and just dance because all we've got is this moment. You down?"

They offered me mostly begrudging looks, but that's the common response to most of the things I encourage or facilitate. I'm used to being a pusher. *Time's limited, people,* I thought to myself. *Let's get over ourselves and into some fun, weird shit!*

I guided them through the simple dance moves of the chorus, and a few butt kicks and low punches later, the whole group's energy was brought to an elevated state. For years, that song has been a staple at my workshops, seminars, retreats, and weekly classes. I'm known for this hilarious, high-energy, cheerleader-style dancing; it's a template that I can use to make it my own. I know if dancing makes me feel more comfortable, then it will most likely make others feel comfortable, too—I can't be the only one. I like the predictability of an unpredictable world.

As we sat down on our granite and oak seats, I could feel that sweet lingering vibration of adrenaline and endorphins in the air. Everyone's lips were turned up in a half-smile, happy that it was over and feeling the rush of dopamine that movement creates. The first layer of awkwardness had been shed.

Recognizing that I wouldn't get this moment back, I took a mental picture, trying to hold onto it for as long as possible.

Everything ends. Everything is fleeting. Everything fucking dies. The only thing that's certain is fucking uncertainty. Don't forget the smell of the fresh pine, or the silence so quiet, or the humming of the earth beneath your feet, Katie. I turned my thoughts back to the group before me and began speaking again.

"Sitting here, on this rock, looking down, you can take a reflective breath. The journey has been both difficult and easy, yet you have still come a long way. Where you are on this rock, where you are right now, was once a place you had dreamed of being as well. Who you are right now was once a dream you had made for yourself, so soak that in. You're okay, and you're right where you need to be." I ended my meditation peacefully.

I sat marinating in all the goodness of my mountain climbing visualization. A few years ago, I had anxiety about the future, so I'd created that visualization to deal with everything that was changing and out of my control. This meditation helped me remember that I have the tools I need to be okay right now, no matter what "gift" the world has for me.

I opened my eyes to my students, and the previous looks on their faces had melted into contentment. They were gleefully in their own mindscape, watching their personal journey; I had set the ball up for them, and they had hit it out of the park. Thousands of thoughts I'll never know flew through their minds, on what I hoped was a journey of self-inquiry. Fuck, for all I knew, they could have been thinking about a bug biting their butt cheek or the kombucha waiting for them at the bottom of the ski lift.

Regardless, my smile could have lit up ten mountaintops; I had climbed my own mental mountain to get to this career milestone, and I was going to soak that shit in. I wiped a tear away from my right eye, only to see the red American flag lines smeared on my hand—but not even a smeared face could take me out of my elevated state.

The shock of my hot steering-wheel hand warmers brought me back to my Kia Sportage, outside the urgent care a month later. I glanced up again in the car sunshade mirror. *Blink, bitch. Blink!* My right eye rolled back into my head and eye socket, but the lid was placid, stuck like a botched Botox job. The cornea wanted to protect itself, so my eye just rolled back instead of blinking. If it weren't for the constant tears filling my eye socket, my eye would have definitely dried out. *Shit, Katie, you need eye drops. Your eye is fucking stuck open.*

You know how when they say, "Don't press the red button," all you want to do is press it even more? I saw my button, knew I shouldn't press it, but did it anyway—I googled "Bell's palsy." Horrific videos of people with limp faces and girls sobbing flooded my iPhone screen. Headlines like, "Paralyzed for Forty Years," "Nerve Surgery," and "Help Me Heal" flashed as top search lines. I quickly locked my screen, at a loss for words.

The blankness of not knowing was better than the exaggerated victim stories of the internet.

My mind floated back to Matthew. It was a Tuesday morning, so he was probably slammed at the brunch restaurant he loved so much, but I had to reach out. With the most compassionate heart and a wingspan that made every hug feel like a jacket, my man could settle any worry. This gentle giant had been cleaning my yoga studio for months before I really saw him. When I opened my eyes and heart enough to notice this Johnny Depp, *Pirates of the Caribbean* look-alike, I found a window into my silly side through him.

Our love story is one for the ages. On our first date, he fell in love with my impulsive, authentic, Jersey girl demeanor. After barhopping in Pacific Beach and a few too many tequila shots (or just the right amount, if you'd asked us then), we stumbled back drunk and madly in lust to my house. I still had college-style bed risers on my *Princess and the Pea* bed so that I could fit all the junk I'd hoarded from those four years at San Diego State. We stumbled past my then-roommate, who was passed out on the couch, and giggled our way into my small, beach-house bedroom.

I remember that our kisses were fierce but playful. He had big lips, big teeth, and a big smile. I loved it. I'd never felt sexy or feminine, but tequila-infused courage gave me the confidence to mount him, playfully unbutton his pants, and start to work my shirt off.

Thank God we didn't turn on the lights. There was just a soft glow through the cheap blinds from my neighbor's front porch light. But in just an instant, I went from what I thought was the sexiest thing alive to the *There's Something About Mary* sequel. What I had gained from my tequila courage, I lacked in balance, literally falling off the bed as I took my shirt off. It felt like slow motion, but the loud thud on impact reminded me that it most definitely wasn't. I can still see him peeking over the edge of the bed, not knowing if he should laugh or help.

"Pretend that didn't happen, okay?" I said with a drunken coy smile and immediately jumped back up to kiss his sweet, stubbled face.

We were magically inseparable for a lust-filled two weeks before he was off to his long-planned trip to Brazil. I was dipping my toes into my first year of international yoga retreats, and he was a wandering soul, so although our travel capacity matched in intensity, it didn't in scheduling. We left with no strings attached, but the six months of our email love-letter writing brought our insatiable love closer. As the emails built up, there was magic in our words and love in our fingers. Two weeks after our goodbye, Matthew wrote:

> *I miss you Katie; more than I thought I would—waaaay more than I'd prefer to, considering the circumstances—but I can't help it, nor do I want to. In the past, I've often hit this point and decided to close myself off, jump ship on my emotions,*

and let my rational mind do the dirty work of severing the relationship, claiming that "It's the right thing to do." My emotional self goes back into the house, makes some tea, pops a Xanax, puts on a record, and continues life in a numb state of blissful ignorance. God bless technology. HUGE heart hugs to you, my princess. Goddamn, you looked great last night!! ;)

Sincerely with love,

Matthew

My heart was never so full. We spoke the same mutual lust language, and I rendezvoused last-minute with him in Argentina after a client gave me her free Delta buddy pass. We spent a magical eight hours in Chicago on my extended layover to New Jersey on his birthday, just so that we could meet his family. The world kept pulling us together, and we kept saying "yes." The continued notes back and forth made my soul light up.

Hi, my beautiful man. Pretty much every second, I find situations that I would want you to be by my side. I think on the way home, my dad knew how sad I was, so he let me fall asleep in the backseat of the car on his lap. I haven't done that since I was a kid...not that he would have ever told me not to, just that I was never emotional enough to need to do it since then lol.

I miss everything about you right now. I miss your reassuring smile, the silly tilt your head makes when you have a shy glance and a smile, the ability to text-fest you at any point to receive and give love, your beautiful, perfect hands that are so soft but strong around mine, your grip from your arms that's so tight, your ridiculous, wonderful ideas to change flights two hours before you take off for another country...your big beautiful dreads, your fuzzy head that puffs up after we get crazy in each other's bodies, your chest hair that warms my heart...perfectly aligned! :-) I want to make perfect babies one day—long from now—and run wild with you as my partner in adventure. Okay, stream-of-consciousness tangents. I can't wait to touch your face again, my knight, my king, the ultimate commanding deck of my heart.

With love,

KB

My eye started to tear up again, most likely attempting to protect the cornea again. The slobber dribble on the right side of my face brought me back to my iPhone 5.

Text him.

Can I get away with not seeing him until this heals? How do I hide this? Can he love a face that doesn't smile?

Text him.

I looked in the mirror and used my right hand to close my top and bottom lip together. *I can't even close my lips to kiss him!* I started to shake as the shock lifted for a moment. *Ujjayi* breathing wasn't going to help me now. The right side of my face started pounding like the blood was rushing to only that side, and I suddenly had the urge to both poop and vomit at the same time.

How can life flip on a dime so quickly? One minute, I was a Wanderlust hot-shot, and the next, I woke up paralyzed. *Don't spiral, Katie.* My mind was reeling as I went through all of the people who would leave me because I was paralyzed. Their faces ran through me like a movie trailer, watching as my family, my friends, and my job left me because I couldn't smile or blink. *Goodbye, Dad; goodbye, InnerStrengthYoga; goodbye, mentors; goodbye, Lululemon; goodbye, Wanderlust; goodbye, Instagram followers; goodbye, happiness. Katie B. Happyy, motivational speaker and self-help guru, is now Katie B. Broken and Katie B. Paralyzed.*

A car beeping at a truck driving by smacked me back into reality like a boot camp, and I quickly texted Matthew.

"I just got out of urgent care and found out I have something called Bell's palsy. I've lost motor function on the right side of my face; a nerve is impinged. The doctor just told me only 80 percent of people get their motor function back, and I'm kind of freaking out. WTF, I'm getting antibiotics now that aren't proven to help, but hopefully, it goes away within a few weeks." My words felt dry and negative, but I didn't know how else to be right then.

He must have digested it, looked it up, and maybe had a little freak out of his own at work. A few minutes later, he texted me back, "You're special, but you're not that 20 percent special." I rambled a few more texts about an acupuncture appointment being necessary right away, and he responded, "I love you so much. Call me when you're done with your acupuncture."

Driving seemed ridiculous. How do you focus on anything other than someone telling you that you're possibly permanently paralyzed? To an outside observer, one would think 80 percent was great. Truthfully, it's just like when you get a review at your job, and although they most likely give you 80 percent of the things you're doing so wonderfully, you only hear the 20 percent room for improvement. I would catch glances of my perma-Eeyore face in the visor mirror. The unmoving right eye created an eerie frozen look, neutral and indifferent.

I found the closest acupuncture on Google in Mission Beach. As I entered the reception, the office manager, a gorgeously sun-kissed twenty-year-old, smiled her bright whites up at me. She sheepishly giggled as she saw me, barely looking at me.

"I'm so embarrassed about my smile," she said shyly. "I just got

Invisalign, and I don't recognize myself. I'm sorry if I sound weird," she trailed off, obviously not the one who booked me on the phone.

I stood speechless in the entranceway, realizing yet again that we are all narcissists when it boils down. I just grunted an approving sound towards her, and the acupuncturist came to greet me with a giant hug, ushering me into her room.

"Let me look at you," she says, her smile reassuring mine. "I Insta-stalked you before you came. You're a pretty great motivator. One of your Monday mantras said something like, 'This breath is a gift, not a given,' right?" The fact that she even cared enough to do her research and was holding me in a half hug brought my emotional body to its knees. That mantra was about my mom, and for my mom. Even moms come and go; I so wanted mine right then.

"Well, gorgeous girl, you're still breathing," she said gently as she held me. "This is just a new, weird normal we have to get used to. The world knows you're beautiful. They won't stop seeing it. You just have to keep showing them."

NAMA-CRAY CALL TO ACTION

1. Change is the only thing that's constant; your circumstances can shift in an instant. The here and now is a gift, not a given, so treasure it.

A. Bow to your intimacy with the moment: it's fleeting. Can you recognize that you won't get it back? Everything dies, and everything ends. The only thing that's certain is fucking uncertainty. How can you honor the moments you have today?

B. Bow to this moment: something allowed you to breathe, so figure out why you got to wake up today. Figure out why you got the ability to smile today because someone else didn't. Where can your smile change someone's day?

CHAPTER 2

Bow to Being Broken and Badass

If manifesting was a sport, I would be the leader on the scoreboard. The entire time I laid on that acupuncture table, I visualized how easy it would be to stand up, look in the mirror, and see my smile again.

Sadly, the acupuncturist had as little knowledge as I did of what Bell's palsy was. I had driven to the nearest one since my Google search explained that the faster you got to Eastern healing, the better the possibility of recovering fully. I didn't do the research to check for a specific acupuncturist; I just booked. I was so lost and vulnerable, and I just assumed that she'd know.

She vigorously massaged my face first, which felt weird, to begin with. We both thought that since my face was paralyzed, it was dead and needed to be woken up. We later came to find out that it was quite the opposite. Bell's palsy is an inflamed, swollen, or compressed seventh cranial nerve attached to the face. It attaches at C7 in the spine and controls the scalp, face, and neck. My face was swollen, like my biceps are after a vanity lifting day at the gym, but this type of swollen wasn't the good kind. The nerve was so inflamed that it couldn't properly fire signals to my face.

I was so grateful there was someone there to help me, even if we just met. Her hands meant to help, but hindsight knows there was nothing she could do. The face muscle massage sensation was deep, and I was going through waves of consciousness, in and out of the pain, visualizing my face miraculously healing in that hour. *Katie, you're stronger than this fire in your face. You're okay. I am a manifesting champion. The world works in my favor (literally faking it 'til I proverbially made it).*

When I stood up, my face actually looked worse. My right eye drooped lower than it had before. I was heartbroken, burying my face into a pile of tissues, only to get dry tissue dust in my eye. I forgot that I had to hold my right eye closed. I sobbed harder, pinching my eyelid closed with my right hand and blowing my nose with my left hand. Drool dripped out on the floor. *Fuck me. How can I teach? How can I be seen with half a face?*

I dragged my feet to my car, Aaliyah the Kia. I started the engine and simultaneously turned on the seat warmers and the air conditioning. *Focus on what's going right, Katie. Just last year, you didn't have seat warmers or air conditioning. You're so lucky. Your yoga mat costs more than most monthly wages in India. You're so lucky. The rest of your body isn't paralyzed. You're so lucky.*

That inner cheerleader was more fake than ever. I couldn't find the light. All my hundreds of Monday mantras couldn't save me now.

I can't wear my contacts. I have to wear my glasses forever. Wait, they fog up in yoga. How am I going to teach with my glasses? Will they approve Lasik for me? How am I going to sleep? How can I keep my mouth shut? How can I keep water in my mouth and drink? How am I going to teach? What do I tell my students?

I couldn't hold it together long enough to call my best friend Tabu, so I texted him simply, "I have an emergency situation; found out I have Bell's palsy today, and I'm trying to hold it together. Can you sub my 4 p.m.? "

"Any thing u need," he replied. Where he lacked in grammatical shortcomings, he made up entirely with loyalty and sass. With a background in dance, Tabu runs on baby food, competition, and lots of caffeine. He personally trains ten clients a day, on top of hours of fitness training for himself, then caps the night by teaching sixty-plus-person, packed yoga sculpt classes at our company, InnerStrengthYoga. I've never been sure if his fiery attitude comes from always being hungry and amped up on caffeine, or if he just enjoys being a bitch.

Tabu and I have similar outlooks on life; although we both love the lives we've created, we're not good at asking for help. I've never been able to be truly vulnerable and empathetic with others. It's something I have tried to break down many times, but the walls come back so hard and fast as soon as someone tries to step in. *Shouldn't people be innocent until proven guilty?* Not with my reactionary self. I am in constant defense and jealousy mode, and everyone is an enemy until they've proven their undying love for me.

I said that I've never been able to be truly vulnerable, and that's true...except with Matthew. We were approaching year four together, and I called him to gain some grounding. There were butterflies so deep in my stomach that my pelvis was tingling, too. This summer was *Bridesmaids* style: between the two of our large Italian families, we attended eight weddings (and were in most of them). Trust me, weddings are never good for year three couples with no rings. Whiskey- and tequila-fueled late-night hotel conversations had turned from fun, light sex to me prodding him for future answers that he didn't have.

I'd always wanted kids. He wasn't so sold. I'd never wanted

to get married, but his lack of sincere and deep commitment made me want the proposal. I wanted to know that he was in this like I was: ride or die. He eventually conceded and gave me the futuristic promise I wanted to hear.

I had big plans for us: a power couple helping the world. He'd already been with me and my self-development travel company to Colombia, Mexico, Italy, Belize, and beyond. We were so good together; we're even good travelers together, which is shocking. *So damn good.* Our families are literally an hour from each other on the east coast, and our parents go to dinners together without us. The Universe brought our spirits together to collide and dance.

"Hey, babe," he answered the phone empathetically. "How are you?" I normally hate that phrase, because it's so generic and without meaning, but this time, I knew he meant it. I broke out in a monsoon of tears, and he sat on the phone and let me sob.

"I got back to my place after work and started researching what we can do," he said. "Did you pick up the steroids and antivirals from CVS yet?"

"No," I choked out. "The ER doctor was so crass. He told me that there's no ppppprooof..." I trailed off, realizing that I couldn't say the P sound. Sobs. Matthew just sat with me, and I could feel his energetic hug through the phone.

I used my right hand to hold my lips together and kept going. "He told me that there's no proof that the antivirals even work. He said there aren't enough studies on Bell's palsy to know the real cause. Western medicine thinks it's viral and lays dormant in the system, like chicken pox. When your immune system gets taxed, the theory is that the virus infects and inflames the nerve. They just put me on steroids for the inflammation and antivirals just in case, and they tested me for Lyme disease as a maybe factor. I'm going to stop at CVS before my eight o'clock Vinyasa class."

"Babe, you're teaching tonight?" he questioned. "Are you sure?"

"I can't sit around. I'm going nuts. I have to be with my people."

"Okay. In my research, eastern medicine believes that it's an imbalance in the inner wind. Basically, it's saying you have too much qi energy...yang energy...stress. The articles say you should calm down and produce more depth and thickness...more yin energy. I know it's the hottest weekend of the summer, but I'm headed to Trader Joe's right now to grab ingredients for some hearty beef stew. Dr. Zhang Li highly recommended it to calm the inner wind. I'm going to grab all the gauze and eye ointment, too. You get your 'scripts, teach, and then meet me at my apartment after."

I tearfully agreed, then hung up the phone. I felt so held by that beautiful hairy man and his actions. *My fucking hero.*

A few hours later, I stood outside my classroom. *Take a deep breath, Katie; you can do this.* I pressed my hand against the hot yoga studio wall, feeling the subtle vibration of the music in the classroom and the drums from the recording studio next door. *One breath at a time.* Heat swung at my face with the door, and the darkness of the room was calming to my paralyzed face. Lit up by fake, dim yellow candles, I felt hidden and safe.

"I'm Katie buBee, thanks fuuuhor joining me fuuuhor your Vinyasa class tonight. Let's start in child's pppfose." Upon hearing the lack of control I had on the right side of my lips, tears started to stream down my cheeks. *Katie, hold it together.*

Bell's palsy is such a messed-up name; the inability to close your mouth prohibits full pronunciation of the F, B, and P sounds, so you can't even tell people what you're suffering from without utter embarrassment.

I pressed my right pointer finger and thumb against the right sides of my lips to hold them together, allowing me to speak my F, B, and P sounds confidently. *Holy fuck, I'm going to be like this forever.* There are so many F, B, and P sounds in fitness. Forward fold, face, feel, *balasana*, boat, be, brave, place, put, plank, peacock, *prasarita*, frog pose, *any* pose. I shook my head hard, trying to shake those thoughts out of my head. I was not going to jump down that rabbit hole.

Just two days before, my biggest stressor was that the number of people attending my classes had dropped from sixty to fifty. My ego loved the numbers, and my ego loved that people loved me. When they didn't show up to class, it felt like they didn't care. I even did two extra workouts that week because my insecure thoughts told me that students follow strong and fit teachers. My small world two days ago felt like it was shrinking with my class size, and my ego believed my relevance was dying with it.

I thought back to the brief moment of jealousy when I saw Tabu's class yesterday, filled to capacity at sixty-five yogis, and I felt so much shame. I blushed, remembering the millisecond where I even coveted his 6 percent body fat. *Why do I value myself on an arbitrary number of yogis attending my classes? Why do I let numbers define my importance?* Being human is so strange. I'd do anything to feel that as my biggest stressor now. Any ounce of superficiality or meaningless worry had been paralyzed that morning along with my face.

My first attempt to say "Inhale, bbbuhbend your knees; exhale, fuhrward fuuufold at the top of the mat," sounded like I was trying to blow up a balloon, and my lips kept slipping on my spit.

"Hang loose in your spine, relax your face muscles, take the tension out of your neck. Let the natural weight of your torso be like medicine, releasing your lower back and hamstrings. Take a horse blubber breath at the bottom, breathe in, and let your lips release and vibrate." *Well, that's a silver lining. I can naturally do horse lips.* I started to pick up a little energetic momentum and held my lips together in the back of the room.

"Try it again, this time with so much ffffforce that saliva falls into your nose!" The whole class got louder, and a silly student even added a "neigh" sound at the end. Giggles spilled throughout the upside-down bodies. *Comic relief, Katie. It's not that serious. You didn't have a stroke. You're alive. Slobber all over your damn self, Beezy.*

My tough-love yelling to myself seemed to carry me through the remainder of the class. As sweaty students emerged from the dark room, I aimed to keep my face neutral, with no smiling attempts, so fewer people would ask about it. If I sagged the left side of my face into a resting bitch face, both sides equaled out. *Who would have thought my RBF would ever come in handy?* To my dismay, too many regulars knew my smile, and there was no hiding it.

"Katie, did you have dental work done?" Rena asked, genuinely concerned. I shook my head no, hoping to shake away the prelude of tears.

Holding the right side of my lips together, I said gently, "The right side of my face is paralyzed, and for most people, it's temporary." Rena stepped back in shock, and, sensing the explosion of tears dancing to get out, she politely said, "Well, anything you need, just reach out."

I felt walled up. I've never been able to ask for help. I've always been the giver and healer. East coast Italian women are the matriarchs. They protect. They don't show vulnerabilities.

Nina, with her curlicue red hair, walked from the room looking concerned. Already feeling her sympathy, I just burst into tears. Students gathered around and listened patiently, like kids waiting to hear a tall tale from a storybook. As saliva drooled down my right side, my left eye closed to blink, but my right stayed open. If I thought I ugly cried before, my inability to blink or close my lips made it pretty damn fucking ugly, or *f-ugly.*

I gathered my yoga breath, held my lips together, and sat up straight. "I have something called Bell's palsy," I announced to the powwow that had collected around me. "Eighty percent of people get their facial function back, but still, I'm scared shitless."

I tried to smile, holding space for them as it sank in. My half-smile was only scaring them more as they stared at the disfigurement. One student came over and sweatily hugged me, but I couldn't hug back. Another student knelt down and just held my frail hand. Tears streamed down the left side of my face, and they welled up in my dry right eye. It felt weird to have so much pity. I hated the feeling. *Don't fucking pity me. But save me. Fuck this.*

Even though I'm sure they all went home and googled Bell's palsy, I realized that I couldn't keep retelling this story over and over again. My gut told me to speak out. If I had to keep retelling this story with my students staring back at my alien, disfigured face, it would only make my bravery shrivel, and the shock of my paralysis would never soften.

Why does no one ever talk openly about this paralysis? Google informed me I had joined the club with George Clooney, Pierce Brosnan, Angelina Jolie, and over 40,000 people diagnosed with Bell's per year in America alone. Most people have the ability to at least hide in a cubicle or take off work when their face stops working. *What was my lesson, oh sweet, ironic world?* I have to sit in front of 600 students a week, and no matter what, I had to keep showing up.

I hadn't even told my family yet. A little part of me was holding out hope that this wasn't real. *Katie, this is your unique story; there doesn't have to be a WHY. You don't have all the answers, so just be brave and go with it.*

I don't remember driving to Matthew's place, but I do remember collapsing into his arms and sobbing so hard that even his chest hair was wet through his layers of shirts. His big brown eyes were both 80 percent hopeful and 20 percent scared.

"Here's some beef stew for you, honey."

"Thank you," I forced out, sitting down and pretending to eat. I don't want fucking beef stew. There's no air conditioning in his studio apartment, and it's ninety degrees in the last week of August, San Diego's hottest time.

"I think I have to record something, Matt," I said. "I can't face my students and followers and have to keep telling this story." So, we decided to film it right then and there.

The first take, I could barely say "Bell's palsy" without losing my shit. Take two was too factual and sounded completely disconnected. The third try was filled with shaky words, but it had enough vulnerability and enough courage to satisfy me. Just enough power posing in paralysis, not enough to scare anyone but definitely no grace.

"So, I woke up yesterday morning thinking that I had some swelling in my face, and when I went to the doctor, they realized I had something called buuhbell's puuuhpalsy. It's ironic that they named it that, because it's really hard to say when you don't have function in your lips. It's a nerve impingement somewhere in the cerebrrrral cortex where all of my motor ffffunction on the right side of my ffface is gone, so I can smile and lift on the left side. I can't control anything, including blinking. Acupuncture helps it, and I'm doing everything I can..." I paused, taking a huge breath.

"Umm, friends are helping out with that stuff, too. I'm doing everything I need to do. I'm seeing myself in a full recovery. Most people recover and get the full function back in six months, and I'm going to be faster and get my function back."

Taking a tiny, lip-quivering pause, I continued. "Umm, the reason I'm making this video is because...I'm scared. And when I see people and have to tell the story over and over again, it brings up the sensation of being scared. So, what I'm asking when you do see me, be really strong and treat me like you normally would. And don't make a big deal out of it. And see me with a full smile. Visualize me with a full smile, both lips up.

"Live today like it was your last day with a full smile. Do things that make you smile. It's given me a lot of appreciation for people who need healing, so if there's anyone else in your life that needs healing, take a moment to visualize them in a healed space already good. And from there, we can make miracles happen. Thanks."

My tears in that video weren't just representing the shock of Bell's palsy; they were cleansing superficial guilt. This kind of guilt was deep, and it had been churning for a while. For weeks, I had been stuck on being "the best yoga teacher" with the highest numbers in class, working on my six-pack, trying to stand out amongst a yoga social media presence with millions of people doing handstands just like me, making myself unique, and proving to people I was worth paying attention to...only to climax to this insanely random facial paralysis. *Did I do this to myself? I swear if I get my smile back, I won't ever care about numbers anymore. I'll put my spiritual practice over my outer body, and I'll never take my smile for granted.*

The next day, Matthew greeted me with, "I spent a few hours on YouTube today looking up every natural remedy for Bell's." He excitedly handed me a bowl of soup, saying, "The turmeric and ginger in here are anti-inflammatories; can you smell the healing happening?" I waited, unsure of what to say.

"I know you don't like watching YouTube," he said calmly, "so I found a really cool sixteen-year-old kid from England who showed me exactly how to tape your eye so that the medical tape doesn't come up in the middle of the night. He said he's been doing it for months now, and it works great."

Fuck you, I thought. *Fuck my face. Fuck that kid in England. Fuck beef stew.*

Matthew looked back at me with the faintest hint of pity, and I lost it again. I already was born with a "lazy eye" on my left side because the forceps used to pull me out of a C-section gone wrong grabbed me by my left eye. *Fuck you, Bell's palsy. Why couldn't you be on my lazy eye side?*

He walked over to me at the table and kissed all over my

face. He kissed my forehead, my left eyelid, my right cheek, my snotty nose, my broken lips. He held my face in his big hands and said, "You are doing so well. You can do this. We will get through this. Maybe this was given as a way for you to learn how to receive. You give all day to your students, so the world is asking you to say thank you. It's 'receiving and gratitude' spiritual boot camp...things I know you want to work on," he concluded. I nodded my head, still wrapped in his arms.

He picked me up in his long, robust arms and put me on the bed. As he laid me down, I felt so frail, helpless against this new face that was holding me heavy and depressed. I felt like there was so much weight on my shoulders, pulling on the right side of my neck and face. The stress was literally pulling the sides of my mouth downward, opposing the smile lines, but something about his arms made me feel safe. I needed him more than I realized, and at that moment, I needed him both emotionally and physically.

Buck up, Katie! My inner drill sergeant was fierce. *Everyone leaves you in life. You don't need him to get through this; you're strong on your own!* I pushed that voice to the back of my mind as I started to kiss his plush lips; only the left side of my mouth was reacting. He kissed back, and I felt his entire lips miss my open lips and land on my huge teeth, like a sixth-grade Truth or Dare kiss. *React, right side! I command you to close your lips. I command you to kiss back.*

My kissing turned into middle-school French kissing, slobbery and confused. My chin became a collage of wet tears and saliva, and I paused the momentum. I tried closing my eyes to refocus on what I wanted to say but only the left one reacted. *Why can't it be easier to let someone in? Why can't I just need him, and be okay with that?*

It's hard to put yourself out there and take risks. You have to like yourself A LOT to take a shot, to see if you can connect with somebody. It's so hard as a human to be honest with people and speak your truth, because there's a huge chance they're going to say something that you don't want to hear. You're going to fuck up. They're going to leave. Everybody dies. But this paralysis left me no choice; I had to break.

"I want to love you right now, but I just don't know how to kiss you," I said vulnerably. I had to jump, knowing that I was probably going to fail and get hurt. But I was already at rock bottom and desperately scared.

"It's a new challenge for us," he offered bravely, and as he stared down into my eyes, he broke. His tears showered my already wet face as we continued to kiss passionately and awkwardly. I pushed his pelvis away slightly to unbutton his shorts. Putting the weight into his shins, he pulled the seam of my shirt up, then swiftly lifted the shirt to get it all the way over my head. He started kissing from my neck, down my bra line, and down to my pants before taking them off. His lips lasted longer over my chest and he looked up at me saying, "See, this is all the same."

As he entered me soft and strong, I knew I needed him. All of the tough girl, alpha-female act I had been putting on for the past three years with him was crumbling. I felt my entire sexy facade of power and poise rotting at its core. I needed him to affirm to me that this was temporary. I needed him to affirm that my beauty didn't lie in my face. I needed him to hold me up when I broke down, because I knew that there would be a lot of breaking in the future.

"I need you," I whispered to him.

"It feels good to be needed."

NAMA-CRAY CALL TO ACTION

2. **What does it take to be seen and fully show up? Vulnerability is the pathway to real love.**
   A. Bow to your vulnerabilities: they are the pathway to real connection. It's not going to be easy, but it will be worth it. Where can you let someone in?
   B. Bow to your fears: being truly seen in all your f-ugly is the only way out. Who deserves to see all of you today?

CHAPTER 3

Bow to LFG: Let Fucking Go

Twelve days, eight hours, and fifteen minutes post-diagnosis, I woke up with the same catastrophic hope I had been waking up with for the past eleven mornings. You know that feeling you get when you wake up from a bad dream, grateful to be awake? It was the opposite of that. I felt my face...and *fuck. Fuck. Fuck. Fuck. Go back to sleep, Katie. It's not real.*

The humming of the bedroom fan swept through Matthews's beach town studio apartment. I could see the morning light peeking through my navy-blue eye mask. As I rolled over, I noticed something different, almost dry. *Shit, my eye is open! Shit shit shit.*

The medical tape and eye goop we had amateurishly applied

last night had come off my eyelid, merely acting as a tent for my eye instead of holding the lid down. *How many hours had my eye been open? Am I blind? My eye has definitely dried out. Fuck fuck fuck!*

Tears—the Universe's natural dry-eye solution—started to stream down my face. I wanted to wake up healed. I wanted to wake up and have my lips close, my eye blink, my cheek crinkle, and my eyebrow lift. I opened my mask up, took the unhelpful tape off, and rolled over to see Matthew.

"Let me look at your face, babe." He rolled over, lovingly tracing his hands down my cheek. "Try moving your lips or your eyes." The reaction on his face told me I was depressingly unsuccessful. "Well, the good news is that you get to be an inspiration today."

My soaked and crooked eyes looked back at him with anger and frustration. I didn't want this kind of inspiration. I didn't want anyone to see my face. I checked my video from the night before, which was at 14,000 views on Facebook and had many comments. My phone blew up overnight, and every icon and app was in the red. I barely had enough confidence to talk to Matthew about my paralysis, let alone respond to all these people.

One breath at a time, Katie. Go to acupuncture. I washed half my face, in fear of getting soapy water in my stuck-open right eye. As my toothbrush revved its battery-powered engine, my saliva flung like a sprinkler from the right side of my mouth. *Shit, Katie. Take things slower.* Not being able to control this timeline was killing me. *Have I ever really been in control?*

Now, acupuncture was the main recommendation from people who had been healed of Bell's palsy, and knowing that it had worked for some made it feel like I was doing something to help my healing. It was a thrilling experience walking into Dr. Zhang Tom's office; I was taking action, instead of sitting in the helplessness that was eating me up. Her office looked like any other western doctor's office, but it smelled like *moksa*, a burning incense-like wood with healing properties.

The white paper crinkled under my yoga pants as I sat on the examination table. I waited for her while listening to a Deepak Chopra and Oprah meditation on my phone, over and over again, to calm my head.

"Hello," she said in a thick Chinese accent, "I am Docta Tom. Bell's palsy, eh?" she grunted, not looking up from her clipboard.

"Have you worked with this before? I'm really scared." The control freak in me was nervous from my first experience with the super sweet but extremely inexperienced massage therapist.

"Mh-hm," she barely responded, with a far-from-reassuring

grunt. Luckily, from my time studying abroad in China, I had grown a thick layer of desensitized skin over my thin western layer. My mind traveled back to one of my favorite Chinese friends, Xin Zhan, who had casually told me one day that I looked fat. I was momentarily offended before I giggled and asked her to elaborate. "You look bigger this week. Eat less this week," was her response. I quickly learned that in certain cultures, stating a fact isn't meant to be offensive. It's just an authentic observation no different than, "Your shoe is untied."

I laid back, full of fear, on Dr. Tom's table. She barely said anything as she started to prick me with a quick, steady hand. I probably should have told her it was my first time getting acupuncture; my supposedly thick skin only lasted about three needles deep before I started crying.

"Why you cry?" she said, momentarily interested.

"I don't know; it doesn't feel good."

Later, after multiple sessions with different doctors, I realized it was a sweet combination of me not wanting to be poked by a tiny, cold doctor, and her heavy-handed old school techniques. But at that moment, I felt abused: pricked by some old Asian lady I didn't know and pricked by this facial paralysis that I *definitely* didn't want to know. I felt like every poke, although aimed to help balance my body, was poking at the few places

I had left that were acting "strong" and holding it together. Every poke was a tiny nudge from the Universe saying, *I told you to slow down!* Poke. *See? You cared too much about your looks.* Poke. *You cared too much about yourself.* Poke. *You're going to lose Matthew.* Poke. *You're never having kids.* Poke. *You're fake.* Poke. *Your followers can see through you.* Poke.

The flood gates had opened. Dr. Tom had prepared more places to put the needles, but she ended up slowing down and backing off due to my inability to slow my ugly cries. Excuse me, the paralyzed f-ugly cries. Now with over twenty needles in my face, ears, toes, belly, hands, fingers, I was hardly able to wipe my tears. At least the tears were keeping my eye lubricated.

"You have too much qi. Not enough blood," my Asian Yoda said poignantly. "Rest. Calm. Build your blood back. More yin, less yang." *Great, another person telling me to fucking slow down.*

How did I get here? I had lost total control of a life I thought I was in the driver's seat of. Me, Katie B. Happyy, someone who manifested a perfect partner into fruition. Someone who was making $80,000-plus doing something I loved, living the dream, teaching fitness, yoga, and CEO of my company b_inspired, having guided over 100 people on international retreats with hundreds more on the roster for 2015. I eat clean, I value eight-plus hours of sleep a night, I love hard, sometimes I drink too much tequila, but for the most part, I'm way more organic than 99 percent of the world.

The salty tears now glistened on the doctor's table, making the white paper disintegrate beneath my head. They represented the fear and lack of control I felt. I was grieving the death of the old me. *I will never again be who I was. This is my new normal. How do I move forward?*

Dr. Tom left the room for me to sit with the needles all over my body to "build the blood and calm the qi," or whatever the fuck. I laid there, so alone, fearful, and powerless.

Fear is imagination undirected. It's always going to be a player in our lives, but we have to decide how much of it is allowed in. My imagination was going to all of the worst possible scenarios, including one where I was alone, childless, and in a mental institution (cray-cray spirals).

I wasn't ready yet to bargain for a new normal, and I wasn't going to accept that my face would be permanently stuck open. Although improbable, spontaneous recovery was my desperate manifestation. My phone pinged an alert, notifying me that it was six hours until my flight to Iowa with Matt to meet his high school friends for the first time. *How serendipitously ironic, Universe.*

Jack, Matt's best high school friend, was getting hitched. I was mortified. My things were packed neatly in my carry-on, boarding passes checked in, and everything perfectly organized to fly...everything except my emotional landscape. *Miracles happen, Katie.*

Something in my gut knew that I wasn't going to heal that quickly. Almost like I deserved more time. My heart screamed at the Universe, God, and my body to heal. I could feel a tiny tug, down to my molecular makeup, that it wasn't time. I would still keep hoping, though; I know how miraculous our bodies are. I wasn't going to let my addiction to control get in the way of the growth I could have by meeting these old friends, but fuck, did I have to swallow my pride. I kept chanting to myself, *"LFG. LFG." But instead of the normal, "Let's fucking go," like I'd chant to hype people in my classes, I changed it to "Let fucking go."*

Those past few days, I'd been winning the "resting" game. Every time I would normally work out, I instead went to a healing session, from acupuncture to cranial sacral therapy. To my dismay, miracles didn't happen on the acupuncture table, and I left feeling the same. I spent the hour watching the spiral of thoughts fly by, playing with my faith. The only thing I had control of at that moment was visualizing my face fully healed by the wedding trip.

After the session, I unlocked Aaliyah the Kia to get in and sulk.

"Hey, excuse me," I heard from across the cars, in a thick

German accent. I looked up to see a blonde girl, around my age, coming over towards me with her yoga mat. Something was different, yet familiar about her. *Fuck,* I realized, *she has Bell's palsy, too.*

"Hey, I'm sorry. I overheard you talking to Dr. Tom. I also have Bell's palsy," she said with a compassionate voice.

"Yeah, I've had it for two weeks now, but I've heard cases where people healed from it that quickly! I'm hoping to just wake up one of these days, and it's all gone," I said, over emphatically, like I was trying to convince myself, too. Patience has never been my thing, and I was word-vomiting all over this girl, the first person I'd met with Bell's.

"I've had Bell's since I was a kid," she said quietly. "I was in a car accident, and it impinged my nerve." I was so uncomfortable around her, and the thought of looking like this my entire life made me antsy. She sensed my unease but barely moved.

"I can tell you have something to share. The secret, though, sweet girl," she took a breath as I hung onto every one of her German-accented words, "is knowing your inner beauty. Don't let anyone ever tell you what beautiful is. You get to define that. Make them love you so much that they can feel your smile, even if you can't see it."

My body felt frozen. *Her whole life?* She looked so not normal.

What? How? I can't do that. I have to hold onto hope. I'm healing. But what if I don't? What if I'm that 20 percent? Fuckin' fuck my f-ugly face.

She went in to hug me, her yoga mat acting like an arm extender to create a larger-than-life hug. I hugged back, I think. She turned and walked away confidently. I never saw her again.

Her words echoed through my mind as I boarded the plane to Iowa. *Don't let anyone ever tell you what beautiful is.* It's a simple notion that's easier said than done, and even more difficult to implement. But as I mulled over that phrase, I began to realize how much potential one person's words have to change the trajectory of your life. It's so easy to give a compliment or say uplifting things, and I'd never known how far that can take someone's life. How the route could divert based on one simple comment.

Her words kept echoing on the wedding party bus the next day in Arkansas. Alcohol is inflammatory to the nervous system, so I wasn't drinking. My nerves were on high alert, and my patience was lower than my self-esteem. *Make them love you so much that they can feel your smile, even if you can't see it.* How can I get them to love me when I'm so embarrassed by what I look like? This isn't how I was supposed to meet his friends. I can't smile. My old tortoiseshell glasses clashed with the lime green "Rent the Runway" dress I was wearing.

Matthew was getting silly on the bus's stripper pole, and I couldn't even laugh at him, physically or emotionally. My fucking face didn't work, and I was so bitter and angry inside. *I'm so tired of being hopeful. I'm so tired of trusting the Universe's fucking path.*

I was 50 percent of my best self, and I still had 50 percent of my face the whole weekend. I didn't dazzle. The pitiful looks from his friends were enough for me to want to crawl back to California and never leave my bed. I used everything I had to keep a straight face. *Ha, the irony.*

When you have nothing to pull from, when you dig deep and there's nothing left, all you can do is surrender. I'd been competing with the Universe, pretending that I was in control. I had bought into the illusion that I had any control at all through prayer, hope, and manifesting. It's all bullshit. I didn't have anything left in me to fight this emotionally or energetically.

Maybe this is my new normal. Let's move right along to the acceptance phase, Universe, shall we? It felt fake, but I had nothing left. The way I saw it, I had two choices: fear or faith. My brave heart had to choose faith. Life happens **for** you, not **to** you, right? *I will define beauty from my core, not my mouth. I will inspire acceptance in the hearts and eyes of my followers.* Or at least I'd try, fail, and then try again.

I want to reference two of my favorite current day prophets' advice: "If fear is imagination undirected, then faith is imagination directed." (Thanks, Tony Robbins.) Or straight from the 305, "You know what spreads faster than any virus? F.E.A.R. When it comes to fear, you can forget everything and run, or face everything and rise." (Pitbull, please perform at my fortieth birthday party.)

I remember thinking that my mom was so stupid to read from the Bible and pray. According to my calculations, God isn't real. Reality to my fourteen-year-old self was just what was in front of me; things I could taste, hear, see, and smell. Praying to an imaginary, all-knowing, all-loving, all-healing God was a cop-out.

Sitting in a reality that I was failing to understand, much less accept, I started to see a touch of why Mom resorted to God. The reality she was creating, to have faith in a bigger power and order, was a more pleasant one to live in. We can't prove if God exists, so why stress about it? If it feels nicer to believe in it and be held by that theory, then live your life feeling good. Who the fuck cares what happens after?

I hated this new reality, but my hate wasn't helping. It's exhausting to be mad all the time. *Let's try faith, Katie,* my inner voice whispered. *LFG—let fucking go. It can't hurt.* Even though I couldn't see ANY reason why I got Bell's, I still trusted that there was a greater purpose for the story. That I still had thousands of unknown people to influence, thousands of half-smiles to inspire, and I became slightly encouraged to see what the world had in store for me. I don't know if it was actually courage; it was probably just me being so fucking depleted that I had nothing left to do but surrender.

A little part of me knew, deep down, that my parents had prepared me for this. With their insane love and support giving me full faith in who I was, I knew I could still love myself and stand in front of people with this broken face. My ego could handle it. I loved more than just my body and my looks; I just had to figure out how to find them again.

And so began my journey home, back to a "me" that was buried under society's expectations, high class attendances, Instagram likes, and Wanderlust festival dreams. Once I finally realized that the idea of control is just an illusion, all I could do was give up and watch the world do what it does. I surrendered to what was given, trusting that although it's not what I wanted, it's what I needed, even if I can't understand why quite yet.

NAMA-CRAY CALL TO ACTION

3. It takes courage to choose faith over fear. A courageous heart knows not to compete with the flow, even if it's not what you asked for.
    A. Bow to faith in your path: it's a way to reach inner contentment in what's given. Get out of your own way. Where are you fighting life?

B. Bow to trust: it's easier to see bad than good, so be courageous enough to see the good. Don't let it be a boulder in your way; keep going until it feels like a fucking stepping stone. Why not create meaning and move forward?

CHAPTER 4

Bow to the Breakdowns

For a tiny Jewish woman, Ms. Hein looked tall behind her teacher's podium, her 1950s hair perfectly coifed. *Just watch the poster.* The words on the elegantly taped poster at the front of her podium were barely visible in my now blurring vision: "If you can read this, thank a teacher." The irony of that statement would have been laughable if I wasn't so fucking hungry. Praying for the bell to ring, I just kept repeating the first few lines of the affirmation, "If you can…" My stomach cramped, and time stood still. I hadn't eaten since lunch yesterday.

Typically, I was enthralled with Ms. Hein's words. The way she choreographed our eighth-grade honors English class felt like an easy dance to me. Because I loved poetry as much as she did, I easily slid my way into the teacher's pet seat. Because I was fascinated by the horrors of the Holocaust and the atrocities her family made it through, we held a strong bond that kids would jealously tease me about once the bell rang. Her stories of their survival always felt so real to me, like they were my own stories.

She doesn't need to know that I'm starving; she would be so upset. I know I can do this; it's worth looking good. The pain is worth it in the long run. I was starting to see stars.

Beep beep beep! The middle school bell rang, giving us the liberating feeling of running to lunch. I zipped up my Jansport, put my colored pens away, and took lunch into the big mess hall. Sixteen popular eighth-grade kids surrounded me at lunch; still, I somehow felt completely alone. *I hope they don't hear my stomach growling.* I ate my cookie in tiny nibbles, consciously taking my time to suck any remaining cookie out of my braces, grasping every morsel I could. It was all I was allowing myself to eat that day, so I savored every bite. I loved controlling the calories and playing with my tipping point of fainting.

I started in on the main event: a bologna and cheese sandwich on white bread with extra mayo. I took a gentle bite and chewed it exactly forty times. White bread = one; braces = zero. I knew when I made the sandwich this morning that it would be frustrating to eat, so I wouldn't have a problem trying to get rid of it. I looked right and left for the volunteer lunch aides, made sure my friends Kaylee and Cari were distracted, then spit it back into my brown bag. I took in three-quarters of the sandwich this way and left the remainder in the plastic bag, making it look like I had eaten most of my sandwich.

Hangry was the best way to describe the final days of my eighth-grade year. Hunger gave me permission to snap at my friends, my teachers, and especially my mom. I wanted a different reason to be angry than what the world had dealt me, so I created it. I decided to be anorexic. *Pain was pleasure, right? You can't get stronger without tearing down muscle fibers anyway. Duh.*

"Have you written your speech?" Kaylee asked, running to my side with excitement. My lifelong best friend could have been a *Limited Too* model. I visualized her and her "cool mom" at the mall, happily buying everything they wanted, then going for TGI Friday's afterward for the trio sampler. Her rose-colored lunch bag filled my face with red envy.

I gave her a defensive shrug, not giving anything away. *Um, duh, Kaylee; I've been practicing every night in my room, but do you think I'd tell you that?* "I've written some parts of it. I'm not too worried about it," I offered nonchalantly. *You're the only other one giving a speech. Mine will be definitely better than yours.* My right shoulder lifted to hide my face. *Cool and calm, Katie. Don't let anyone know your secret.*

"I've been working on mine with my mom all week. Bryan

helped me write and rewrite it. Since he gave his eighth-grade graduation speech, I guess he thinks he has some authority to change mine. Like his was some big success or something..." She trailed off, trying to joke with me about her nerdy brother. I wasn't even present enough to get her joke; my rumbling stomach was a welcome distraction. *Here come the stars again.*

"Aren't you like, so totally excited for your braces to come off today?" She gleamed, trying to lighten my threatening mood. Staring at her naturally perfect teeth, I responded with a coy "yes."

My gums ached; the braces had been especially tight since my last visit. For what may have been the one millionth time in three years, I ran my tongue over the braces, imagining the feeling of my teeth. *My teeth will be perfect, my speech will be perfect, my body will be perfect, everything will be perfect.*

After school, Dad took me to what felt like my third home for the past eight years: a tiny house that had been converted into a cozy office. Dr. Wood, my orthodontist, tried to mask her mouth-torture chamber with flower pictures and relaxing fucking music. Years of painful expanders, colored rubber bands, and headgear that made my fourth-grade sleepovers hell, were finally coming to a close. As promised to me since my first visit in second grade, today was the day my straight teeth made their debut.

As I peered up into the familiar, cold fluorescent lamp, I

couldn't help but be excited. The dental hygienist did her initial check, rubbery fingers and all, then Dr. Wood swept in for her final approval before taking those metal food traps off my face.

"How's your mom, Katie?" she asked. Her voice was muffled through her surgical mask. You could see the glow of empathy tinted with pity in her eyes.

"Fuuuuuuhhhne," I hissed, her two hands deep in my mouth. *Why do they always ask you questions when your mouth is stuck open? Is it some sick orthodontist joke? Like when the day's over, do they compare who had the craziest open-mouth words or who got the most spit on them?*

"She's been in my prayers," she continued. "We're always thinking about her in the office. Tell her that we're thinking about her."

I don't reply, putting up a wall. I'm not going there, not today.

"Well, I'm not too happy with the movement," she says as she starts to pull her gloves off and sits back. "We're going to have to wait another two weeks."

My world spun, my mouth still filled with the taste of her fucking gloves. *You lying bitch; you can't do this to me! I am the student body president who's supposed to be giving her graduation speech tomorrow.*

"You had said I could get them off today," I started, getting a little louder, choking back tears. "I give my graduation speech tomorrow." I couldn't hold back. Hearing my tone, Dad ran in from the waiting area.

"Dr. Wood, she's been counting down the days for months now. Tomorrow's really important. And we've made...special arrangements; her mom's going to be there." The way he paused made me so uncomfortable that I couldn't look at him.

Placing his tanned hand gently on my shoulder, my dad's soft green eyes took the sentimental approach with our orthodontist, the complete opposite of mine. Jim Burke has always been my champion; he will forever fight for me, even if I'm in the wrong.

"Let me take a moment with the file. I'll be back." She takes the file to the back room, leaving my Dad and me to wait. *He will make this better. He always does. Jim Burke fixes everything. He's the damn mayor of our tiny 4,000-person township. He's Superman.* I look up lovingly into his soft, wrinkled Irish eyes, weathered from thirty years of outdoor stone masonry.

Dad (or "Daddy" when I wanted something) grew up as the fifth of six Irish children in Pennsylvania. Being a child of the sixties, and a natural artist at heart, he followed in his siblings' footsteps, experimenting with hallucinogens and more. He loved his father, a successful mushroom farmer, until the day he passed when Dad was sixteen. His father's alcoholism was a huge factor in his pursuit of sculpture at the University of Westchester, and unlike his siblings, my dad fell out of the drug world and into art. He was a talented and respected sculptor, painter, and eventually photographer, which landed him a job at The Camera Shop Inc. where Mary Kathryn Latella, or Kathy, was his boss—my mom.

Mom (or "Mommy" when I wanted something) was the oldest girl of seven Italian Trenton kids. She was only one of two that went on to get any sort of college education, and she prided herself in holding the siblings as together as she could. When Jim Burke walked into her life, she was already months deep into another relationship at The Camera Shop, and her brilliant brown eyes barely saw him. They were close friends, he respected her driven and successful nature, and she respected his easy-going, out-of-the-box-thinking character. They made a perfect combo. Dad's creative side filled our bellies with delicious dinner experiments inside the home he literally built with his hands, and Mom's matriarchal style of love kept our family unit together and strong. Spaghetti Sundays were our specialty. The d'Angelos were a strong unit. Every birthday, anniversary, or any other reason to celebrate started with egg bagels and cream cheese from Tony Romano's, and ended with an ice cream cake from Carvel's.

As Dr. Wood came back into the room, her face started to crease, as if she was about to drop some bad news. "Okay,

Ms. Katie. Against my better judgment, we can take them off today." I looked directly at Dad with my last metal grin of all time. He chuckled his normal reassuring laugh, and once again, the Burkes won. Katie and Jim = one; orthodontist = zero.

When we arrived home, I barely remembered I was starving. My AOL Instant Messenger screen was waiting for me to blast to my closest friends that it finally happened. Those strangely slimy pearly whites were gleaming; I couldn't type fast enough, I was so happy.

"Katie, why don't you go show Mom?" Dad asked gently. I avoided him and kept typing. My impatience was growing with him, the hungrier I got. *No, I don't want to see Mom. I just get annoyed when we talk anyway.*

"I'll go up in a sec," I replied. I could feel his firm stance waiting in the office doorway, his breath making his black mustache hairs dance below his bumpy nose. I sighed frustratedly, then turned to leave, my footprints loudly stomping the hardwood staircase as a warning to Mom that her fourteen-year-old hormonal terror was coming upstairs. Pro-tip: if you want to make a good creaky entrance, you should always walk in the center of wooden stairs; if you need to sneak, then walk along the edges. I'd spent many nights creeping halfway down after learning that trick, listening in to Mom and Dad's conversations secretly.

As I stepped into the room, I accidentally smacked the wood

door into the bed frame behind it. *Shit, Katie. She just got that new temporary hospital bed put in.* Since we were a waterbed family, the hospice workers had to put it in a catty-corner to the waterbed frame. Waterbeds aren't conducive to chemo treatments and diaper changes.

"Hi, honey," her throat sounded dry, "How was your day?" I barely recognized her: the chemo had made her face and fingers puffy and swollen, and her wedding ring needed to hang from a necklace instead. She was equally as frail in other places, like her legs or arms; the muscle had withered down to almost nothing. Her faint smile when she saw me wasn't hiding anything; the dark circles under her eyes told the story of her sleepless nights in pain.

"Fine," I said, purposefully staring at my hand as it grazed the metal of her hospice bedframe. I couldn't look at her, now that cancer had changed every part of her. It was easier not to.

"Let me see your teeth, hon," she said encouragingly. I half-opened my mouth, not willing to share my excitement with her. I didn't want to share *anything* with her. It was easier to pretend like she didn't exist by focusing on what I could control. My stomach growled again.

"Katie, you look beautiful, and your teeth are gorgeous. Ten years, countless visits, and twenty grand paid off, huh?" She chuckled at her own joke, which turned into a choke, causing Dad to come running in to help her regain her composure.

"You okay, Kat?" he said lovingly as he held a hand towel near her mouth as she coughed. She nodded in slow-motion, her neck muscles barely able to do the full range of movement. I noticed that her unpainted fingernails, which were always so well-kept and clean, had turned black and blue underneath, splotched with radiation's aftermath. She wore a compressor sleeve on her left arm to keep the lymph nodes from swelling.

My body language was impatient and self-absorbed; I couldn't be bothered with this. I had people to instant message, and I was hungry.

"Want Dad to get you some food?" she asked after hearing my stomach's growl. "I think he made my tuna pasta salad recipe; there are leftovers in the fridge."

"I'm fine, Mommmm," I said with my fourteen-year-old atti-tude. I was hungry, and I was mad. If I admitted that I was angry about her newly bald head, her frequent extended stays at the University of Pennsylvania Cancer Center, her pathetic weak body, or her faint and fading smile, I would be admitting to myself that she was sick...and that was something I couldn't control. So instead, I decided to distract myself by fixating on my physical body—which was already athletic and thin—by starving myself to see how long I would last. To my fourteen-year-old self, that made total sense.

Dad was so busy with Mom that there was no noticing if I finished my plate, and when I couldn't take the hunger pangs anymore, I'd binge-eat whatever was in my way. After today's visit, that would be an entire sleeve of Oreos. The guilt over the 1,000-plus calorie indulgence felt good...so good that there wasn't space for me to feel or think or worry about anything, especially Mom.

The next day, I was over-the-moon excited for my big moment as president of Queenstown's 2002 eighth-grade class of fifty. As a lifelong believer that I was meant to be a pop singer (fuck Buck's County Playhouse; they couldn't see talent if it hit them in the face), I decided to perform a parody of a song from *The Little Mermaid*.

Flowing in all white, my cap and gown almost matched the bleach blonde Shakira hair I was so proud of. I couldn't keep my mouth closed. *Look, world! No braces. Ten years of nightly pain, and boom! Here I am.*

I walked up, awkwardly adjusting my cap and wiggling on my wedge shoes. *You've got this, Katie.*

"You've got this, Katie!" I hear a faint cheer from the front row, and my eyes catch the wheelchair holding my mom's frail body. She had arrived thirty minutes prior via some volunteer firefighters who brought her on a stretcher to the ceremony. They literally wheeled her in on a stretcher to my fucking graduation. I was mortified...until my stomach growled. *You look good, Katie. Focus.*

"Look at this class, aren't they neat?

Wouldn't you think that we're a class, a class that has... everything?

Look at this group and wonderful school.

How many star students can one class hold?"

I sang the entire Ariel parody acapella all the way through, and when I finished, the crowd cheered with a standing ovation. My mom couldn't stand, though. She could barely clap. I saw her through the corner of my eye, but I ignored her, so deeply embarrassed.

Once technically "graduated," we all dispersed to hug our families and rendezvous in the cafeteria for a potluck-style arrangement of baked goods. Everyone was happily taking photos with their new pink or red polaroid cameras. *It's so cool*, I thought, *we don't have to wait for the film to be developed.* I had saved a month's worth of my six-dollar-hourly wage to buy thirty-six picture opportunities.

Kaylee's mom, Shannon, who was probably a few glasses deep at that point, ran over to us and said, "Kat, I'll take a family photo." My mom shook her head. As a world-class photographer, she never liked being the subject of the photo, much less the sick, bald version of herself. But Shannon's persistence won. My brother, Patrick; my mom's mom, Mary; Dad; and I surrounded her wheelchair as she held the pink roses Dad had gotten for me on her lap. That is the only photo I have of my mom while she was sick, and it's the last photo I ever took with her.

"I'm so proud of you, honey," she said to me just before I ran off to hang with my friends. "You did such a good job." As I left, the firefighters started to put her back on the stretcher.

The following day, Dad dropped Patrick and me off at Aunt Leeanne's while he and Mom went in for a procedure at UPenn. My mom's sister and closest friend happily took us in, always acting like a second mother but with way stricter rules. She loved clean nails, bump-free ponytails, a clean house, and hypo-allergenic dogs that didn't shed.

I had smuggled a hermit crab into my cousin Sara's room without Aunt Leeanne knowing, and I smelled like hermit crab pee. Sara and I giggled as Herbie's claws walked over Aunt Leeanne's off-white carpet, up her bed curtain, and onto the bed. We loved our secrets. Born only six months apart, we were bound to be best friends and sisters.

"Katie!" Aunt Leeanne said as she firmly swung open the door. We jumped up to our feet and spun around, my face flushed bright red. I knew we broke a big rule. *Darn it, Katie. Now look what you've done. We aren't going to be allowed to have any sleepovers anymore.*

But...something wasn't right. Aunt Leeanne's normal disciplinarian face looked more worried than usual. "I'm going to take you two back home now. Your dad called, and he said it's important for you to come home to see your mom."

First relief, then confusion, hit me over the head. I slowly got my overnight bag and traveled the forty-five minutes back to my house with my twelve-year-old brother in silence.

As we pulled up, Aunt Leeanne's Nissan Infinity tires crackled over the steep stone driveway of our Rumble Falls Road property. Dad came to open my passenger side door, saying delicately, "Lee, can you take Patrick inside to unpack?" When she nodded, he turned to me, saying, "Let's take a walk down the driveway to chat a little, huh, Katie?"

I immediately started shaking my head *no*. I knew in my heart what he was going to tell me; I had known for months. But if he didn't say it out loud, then it wouldn't be true. He put his hand on my back as we started walking.

"You know your mom went in for that new trial drug this weekend..." He trailed off, not being able to hold himself together. As his strong voice started to crack, tears ran from my eyes, as if I had turned a faucet on that wouldn't stop for days.

"We had hopes that the drug would slow down her cancer, but..." Again he stopped, losing his breath.

"*How long?*" I rudely interrupted my broken father.

"Three days or less."

My world started to spin. Our words drowned in tears that turned into sobs. *No, no, no, no, no, no. I'd been avoiding her. I'd been avoiding this. If I just looked away, it wouldn't be real. This wasn't the way it was supposed to be. Jim Burke, fix it! No, no, no, you guys always taught me breakthroughs and miracles could happen after breakdowns. Where's the breakthrough, Dad?*

"She needs you to be strong right now, Katie. Her organs are failing, one by one. They have her on morphine, so she isn't in pain at this moment. Go in and be with her."

That familiar cramp from my anorexia suddenly turned into a stabbing pain in my stomach, lungs, and heart. The world started to blur as I walked upstairs to sit in her room with her. A lot of those first hours were spent just sitting and holding her hand in the hospice bed.

Those hours of waiting were nauseating. Different layers of my 100 Italian family members, and 100-plus extended "chosen family," would stop in to bring food and sit with her. The waves of different casseroles and lasagna trays started to feel heavier as time went on. Dozens of Mom's closest people were in our house for those few days mourning, laughing, eating, and supporting.

I was numb. I couldn't do much but hang out with Herbie the hermit crab in my room, and I've come to realize that this was my first real lesson in "sitting in it." None of it felt good, especially since I'd been running from this notion for two years. *My mom was a fucking beast, a superwoman. Nope. Nope. Nope.* And so, we just sat.

Over thirty hours had passed since my dad told me the news, and we were approaching our second night of waiting. I started taking out our old photo albums and looking for any picture of the healthy version of my mom that I could find. It gave me something to do.

About two hours into my photo scavenger hunt, dozens of photos lined the couch in my mom's room. Her eyes opened less and less, but I knew that she knew I was with her.

"What are you doing, pumpkin?" Dad asked.

"Finding photos of mom for the funeral."

"You don't have to do that now," he said.

"Yes, I do." *Don't you realize, Dad, I have to do something, something that I can control? Let me have this, please.*

"I wish she was actually in front of the lens more often; it's all photos of you guys," Dad said, conceding to help and sitting next to me on the couch.

"She is an amazing photographer," the tears started to well up in my eyes. "She *was* an amazing photographer." Changing her life to past tense suddenly made it all the more real. *Why was that so weird?* I broke down.

That night, we made a makeshift bed out of a couch and extra couch cushions so Dad could sleep next to Mom. Her hospice bed was too high and small for him to creep in. After stacking a couple of extra sets of cushions, we just about got him to the bed's height so that he could have one final night with her. My heart was ripping apart thinking of my Dad spooning her for the last time after twenty-five years.

Before saying goodnight to my dad, I asked if I could have some alone time with my mom. He agreed.

"Mom," I whispered, "I know you can't respond, but if you can hear me, squeeze my hand." I waited for a few moments—no reaction. Even though I saw her chest rise and fall, I had to stick my finger under her nose just to be sure. *How can she keep stealing such small sips of air? Every breath was stolen.* The tiny wisps of air crept out her perfect nose.

"Mom, I'm sorry I haven't been nice to you lately. I'm so sorry that I didn't spend more time with you. I've been such a bitch. I'm sorry I fought you about saving 50 percent of my paycheck. I just never thought you were actually going to..." I trailed off, trying not to let her hear me cry.

"I promise you that we're going to be okay here without you. I'll take care of Dad and Patrick and watch out for Grandma and your sisters. We're safe..." I regained my breath. "There's no need for you to be in pain anymore. You can move on."

I sat with her, putting my face on her chest like I remembered doing for so many years. *This is the same chest that fed me, and now the same chest that took her away from me. Fuck breast cancer.* I picked my head up from her heart and looked at her young, forty-three-year-old face. *What was she thinking? Did she feel anything? Was she hovering over her body like in those movies we used to watch on Lifetime? Was she already an angel? Was she just fucked-up on morphine? I wish I were on fucking morphine. Feeling doesn't feel good.* I wanted to feel the pain of starving myself, but I couldn't eat either way.

Ever so faintly, she inhaled and squeezed my left hand. An overwhelming sigh of relief came over me: *she'd heard me.*

"I love you, Mom. We're safe. It's okay to go now," I whispered one more time. Going into it, I wasn't so sure how I was going to be able to leave that room, but I did, almost as if some omnipresent strength came in and lifted me from the

bed. I walked to my bedroom for the last time with my mom in our home.

The next day, on July 1, 2002, Kathy Burke sat straight up for the first time in three days and took her very last breath. Dad grabbed onto her body just in time to catch the bile on his chest; it's as if her spirit flew from her body at that moment. He screamed, my brother screamed, and I crumbled to the floor where I stood. I knew by the sound of the cries that cancer had finally taken her.

I took a few sobbing breaths, then gently walked to her bed. I reached out to touch her leg, but immediately pulled my hand away, as if her body was hot coals. Mom wasn't in there anymore; it was a lifeless corpse. My gaze traced up to her chest. It wasn't moving. The past two days, it had been rising and falling, and for the past fourteen years of my life, it had been inhaling and exhaling. The pain she'd been experiencing for two years was over. The hope she'd held onto, believing that breakthroughs could happen even in the breakdowns, was gone. Now, there was nothing. No breath in, and no breath out. I quickly walked away from her body, not wanting anything more to do with it. From now on, Mom was with me in both my heart and my head.

The Latin root of the word "inhale" is *inspira*, which means "to inspire." We inhale (inspire) and exhale (expire) thousands of times a day, rarely thinking about this automated biological response. At fourteen years old, I watched Kathy Burke, my badass Vice President of Camera Shop mama, take her last breath. I knew that cancer had taken her breasts, but I didn't know that it would take her life. I never realized that she, a strong Jersey woman, was actually going to die. Silly, huh? But watching her chest rise, then watching it fall to never rise again, switched on something inside my little adventurous heart. I remember thinking, "That's it? That's all we are? One final exhale?"

That was my first real lesson in LFG, and it shook me to my core. *That's the grand finale we're always talking about?* A tornado of thoughts spun through me ranging from, "Well, you better get started with the partying," to "Holy fuck, what's the point anyway?"

My hormonal, selfish, fourteen-year-old self didn't know everything. I didn't have the control that my small world led me to believe I did—my mom fucking died. But man, did she fight, and I didn't even notice. The guilt of my self-absorption in my mom's final weeks has weighed on me my whole life. Why did I care so much about my food and not my mom? Why was my AOL AIM chat more important than looking into my mom's dying eyes? Was I just mirroring her fight with my anorexic plight?

The downward spiral of thinking, "If only she had died when I was eighteen—when I could explain my emotions better—

what would it have been like to be friends with my mom instead of fighting with her? Why didn't I know she was dying?" These thoughts have been a guiding driver since that horrible year. The crass Jersey girl in me hates affirmations and common sayings. But for some reason, those were all that I could hold onto. The Universe (or Mom's Catholic God) didn't make a mistake, per se. Some people come into this world to raise the compassion level of the world and those around them. The loss of their presence can bring about an understanding of both yourself and your purpose in this short life. I chose to believe that the pain my beautiful mother went through had a tiny bit of meaning; if nothing else, she went through that for me to write this, to you.

Thirteen years later, and six weeks into my paralysis in 2015, I could feel the same disconnection that I had created from my dying mom. All I wanted was to run from this new normal. By conceding that this may be how I look the rest of my life, I was afraid that the Universe would stop working to heal me. *I can't look it in the eyes. I'd rather be on AIM chat (Instagram now, duh). No, no, nope, nope.*

It had been a good, hard day of coaching and teaching. I was finally back in my physical groove. My face may not have been working, but I was rocking new glasses, doing eye drops every two minutes, holding my big lips together for my Ps, Bs, and Fs, and moving forward with lifting and yoga-ing, because life had to go on. By three o'clock in the afternoon, I was completely exhausted; I'd started my day with a good yoga sculpt class, secretly wishing I could run, but the wind was too taxing on my stuck-open eye. At least the hot yoga room created a space for my eye to have the wet humidity. I drove around University Square to privately train two moms at their homes, hit a corporate account in La Ventura, and added an advanced power yoga class at InnerStrengthYoga. Most of the time, my two o'clock lull came from not being able to stay fully hydrated after teaching several classes. But I had been so good with eating clean these past six weeks: no alcohol, coffee, sugar, salt, or any other things that could make my nerves flame up, so I knew it wasn't that.

Still, that day I was fucking tired, and I deserved a break from "healing," right? I saw a Five Guys burger place and imagining the salty taste of French fries gave the hormones in my stomach a mental orgasm. Ghrelin, the hormone that makes you think you're hungry when you're hungover, sleep-deprived, or dehydrated, was screaming to be noticed.

When the salty, high-blood-pressure basket came out, I doused it in the pump-style ketchup. That sugary, fake tomato sauce looked like pure heaven on earth. I went outside, and instead of hiding in my car, I decided to sit on the curb. I looked around to see if anyone was watching; I'd been eating in private because it was a horrific sight. I had to hold my lips together on one side to keep any food or drink in. There were swollen, cold sore-like bumps from accidentally biting my inner lip that I had no control of. Typically, slobber would drip down the side of my face since I couldn't keep everything in my mouth. Coupled with my pirate eye patch (which was covered by my glasses) and the typical "stay-in acupuncture pressure-point pasties," I looked like the meth heads that ate under the bridges in San Diego with their stolen grocery cart homes.

A flash of my mom, looking sick and pathetic in her hospital bed, went through my mind. I remember intentionally leaving the room when she'd try to eat off her tray at the hospital. As her arms got frailer and others had to feed her, I would get nauseous just by seeing her so helpless. I got so embarrassed and nauseous from the memory while sitting on that curb that I couldn't even eat the French fries. *Fuck me.* I started to cry looking at the cold fries. *What are you doing, Katie? Don't let people see you doing this. Don't let people see you low. Stay strong, buck up. Focus on the positive.*

My inner critic's voice started a battle with fourteen-year-old Katie, who screamed at me: *You got through your mom's passing without noticing her, pretending it wasn't happening. You can get through this. Just close your eyes and pretend. Manifest, bitch.*

For some reason, it was like I was sitting at the "Rock Bottom Café" again, having a familiar cocktail of denial and self-loathing. But this time, instead of ignoring my mom and pretending like that could fix it all, something stirred in me.

I had to sit in the filth, the dirt, the fucking pain to see what was on the other side of the sensation. *Stare into discomfort. Failure happens more frequently than success. We're all decaying and dying, so what the fuck do you care?*

I started to rock back and forth, like someone having a panic attack. My inner critic was tired of being so mean. It was tired of being hopeful and strong. It was tired of pretending that it was going to all work out. It wanted a hug from my mom, to be rocked and told it was going to be okay. It wanted Mom to say, "Katie...eat the damn fries."

Rocking back and forth on that curb, tears hydrating my dry eye, I found myself eating the ketchup-glazed fries. I needed to sit there, sit in that feeling, and be okay with eating the fries. I couldn't take the pressure anymore of being so mean to myself, of living with that denial and stress. It took so much more of me to ignore it.

After I finished eating, there was ketchup everywhere. My lips looked like I had missed the mark with lipstick, a half clown painted on my cheeks. My pace started to pick up; I was stuffing fries into my mouth by the handful. Crying, rocking, shoveling. It wasn't pretty. I wasn't okay.

But I was sitting in it, and I was going to *keep* sitting in it. It was like I was eating away the guilt of running from my mom's pain and ugliness. I was stuffing down potatoes to fill the hole of shame I had been living with for thirteen years. And damn, it was such a big fucking shame hole. When the bucket of fries was finished, I stopped rocking. That voice was singing to me. *You're okay, beautiful girl. You're okay. You're okay. You're okay.*

It felt like a psychotic break, finally realizing that this whole time, I had been trying to control the Universe through manifesting, secretly and narcissistically proclaiming that my vision was better than what was given. I almost felt ashamed all over again, but that sweet, gentle voice was finally starting to get louder than the bullhead inner critic that had been plowing me forward without grace. It felt like that inner voice was finally cheering me on and giving me a break. And fuck, it felt so good not to care so much.

That German girl's voice rang back in my head: "Don't let anyone tell you what beautiful is." I felt a sudden rush of vindication. I knew deep down that one of the reasons I got this paralysis was so that I could show up and be seen. I drove to my next client, The Girl Scouts, and recorded a quick yoga flow on my phone before the session. I posted the video, captioning it with, "Today, I'm grateful that everything else works. #halfsmileisbetterthannosmile."

I immediately started crying again, feeling both relieved and shitty, regretful all over again for not being there with my mom in the way that I needed support now. But at the same time, I felt so happy that I didn't have cancer and that my body worked. Those ugly tears of gratitude mixed with remorse made me puffy-eyed, yet powerful. It was time to be a broken badass and keep sitting in it, to see what came out on the other side.

Energy cannot be created or destroyed, just transformed. So, when I feel irritated, angry, scared, etc., I have to learn to channel that energy to use it for my benefit. I am the only one who will be stuck in my head for the rest of my life, so I have to make sure that it's a nice place to live. Irritation? Go take it out on a run. Angry? Go clean your kitchen. Scared? Go give back to people and volunteer selflessly. Sometimes, I can channel the anger and shame and use it to brighten someone's day. Sometimes, I can channel it to go work out. Sometimes, I can channel it into building empathy and compassion. Sometimes, I get black-out wasted to forget the feeling for a few moments. That's probably why my psycho self went into fitness.

I love watching and feeling the burn. In my yoga classes, during a long hold of a deep revolved crescent lunge, I often implore my students to, "Be brave enough to see what's on the other side of the sensation." The only way muscle fiber can become stronger is if it first tears so that it can call more muscle fiber to the party and repair itself. It's not enough to get stronger abs; breaking down muscle means breaking through to more gains. The burn and pain you feel when weight-lifting or doing push-ups or lunges is a necessity to create strength.

Just like our physical muscles, we also have to tear down our mental and heart muscle fibers. The world is always going to keep throwing shit at us that has the potential to break us down, but what makes life joyful is having the inner strength to sit in the mess, knowing that it will pass. Our mission here on this earth is to keep tearing that muscle fiber; the secret to success is learning how to be in that burn and still see joy and hope even when it doesn't feel good. We have to sit in that ugly fear, sometimes literally with an ugly face, and be okay with the discomfort. The weight we carry can either be used as bricks to build up a wall around you, or as a foundation for the path ahead. Forge forward into the new normal, the different, the wisdom of uncertainty.

NAMA-CRAY CALL TO ACTION

4. **Who you are in the downfall matters more than who you are on the way back up. The practice of sitting in discomfort is a necessary part of life, so trust the wisdom of uncertainty.**

    A. Bow to the breakdown: it creates breakthroughs. Messy is beautiful and sticky and awful and worth it. They didn't say it would be easy, but they said it would be worth it. Where can you add trust to a current breakdown?

    B. Bow to the Rock Bottom Café: at least from there, the only way to go is up. Where are you excited to break through and move forward?

CHAPTER 5

Bow to Your Story

My happiness was dwindling. *How long could I keep this "I'm okay; I'm a powerful paralyzed woman" act up? I missed feeling sexy. I missed my life.*

Now, countless weeks into my paralysis, I started to ask for my mom's guidance and help. I wanted to keep channeling that voice that kept saying, "You're okay," and not the one that wanted to fight back. I needed to make sense of this paralysis and its divine timing. But I was so goddamn angry. Impatience was starting to turn into daily anger. The seeds of hope I'd been planting weren't growing as I wanted.

Whether it was pity, love, or a mocktail of both, Matthew and I moved in together that month. The union gave me momentary seeds of happiness, but it was fleeting. The thrill of someone else's choices dictating my happiness wasn't lasting. Katie B.

fucking Happyy couldn't find her happiness. Good. So, let's try another angle. At this point in my life, I'd already figured out that life would answer my questions; I just might not have been asking the right ones or, even better, I didn't like the answer I was getting.

People who are naturally bubbly and happy piss me off. I'd spent most of my life hating them and judging their fakeness, so when I'd meet the few who were completely genuine in their optimism, I would distance myself as if they were a warlock or a witch. Worse, the ones who are tragic optimists can't actually see the world for what it is: a wasteland of human suffering with people just trying to make it. *Nope, not me, world. You're not fooling me.*

Being a big results-oriented boss bitch, I had set my sights on five profitable international retreats that year. It was a big number for my very green leadership, and the Bell's palsy had beaten my normal "crushing sales" spirit down hard. Enrollment was low for my October trip to Ensenada; I had been trying to rebuild my self-confidence enough to host a retreat, let alone convince twenty-five people to attend.

Sitting at the computer that day, I felt the bottom line weighing on me: no attendees, no smile, no hope. I grabbed my phone to aimlessly scroll my Instagram newsfeed, pretending that was going to give me any gratification. *Let's see who's doing better than me today. Fuck you, Kaitlyn, and your cute family. Fuck you, Derek, and your hot dad bod. Fuck you, Ariana; I don't care that you lost ten pounds.*

I was deep in the endless scroll of self-pity when suddenly an email dropped from Amelie, the regional Lululemon director:

"Katie—You've been selected as a regional ambassador to be in our Spring 2016 International Collection. Our production team is looking to work with you for an upcoming Women's Power Yoga shoot in Beverly Hills on Friday, Dec 11, for the full day.

"In addition to being the main website banner for women, we are looking to do an 'UNDERWEAR' photo banner when we shoot on Thursday and wanted to check in with you about this. Would you be comfortable with an underwear shoot? These are full bum undies, of course."

I finished reading and re-reading that email ten times, in complete shock. *Wait, what? Don't they know I have Bell's palsy? I can't be an international model for their website!*

Somehow, the email made me cower even lower into my desk chair. I'd have to email them and explain the situation. They had probably seen an old photo of me. Seeing that I couldn't get myself out of the comparison victim hole I so desperately loved being in, I showed Matthew the email for some outside validation.

"Holy shit, babe! This is so cool. This is definitely something to look forward to."

His answer wasn't the one I was hoping for. I wasn't looking forward to it. I was mortified by my outer shell and didn't want to be the main attraction on an international website geared towards selling hot clothing to the most beautiful people in the world. *And an underwear model?* Don't they know my old daily ritual of squats as a prayer to my perky butt had turned into a daily ritual of laying on an acupuncture table as a prayer to a perky face? *I sag everywhere, Lululemon! My butt **and** my face.*

Things were dropping into my life that were good, but I was resisting them. I went out for a brisk walk, the angriest one I could muster. Running was impossible, because if I taped my eye shut to run, I'd get too dizzy to see straight. My thoughts fantasized forward to me giving up this once-in-a-lifetime opportunity and hating myself for it. *What if my face has healed before then?* My mouth started to water with the imaginary sensation of my future self-loathing. *No. I can't give this up.* My anger and my hurt were bubbling up. If I couldn't be happy, I had to find a new direction to swing—I had to ask a different question.

The adrenaline of my rage made me take out a note in my phone and start voice recording my thoughts. I was sick of my own bullshit. If I couldn't create happiness, then I sure as fuck could live with purpose. I could live as if this opportunity didn't have meaning, or I could act as if it did. I'll never know if it was a "woo-woo divine god" thing, but I could surely force myself to look at it that way. I started talking angrily into my voice note:

"I'm fucking ready to take full responsibility for the experience of my life. I'm fucking ready to expand the quality of how I live. I'm fucking ready to feel again and to create depth in my relationship with myself and what's given. I remember feeling happy—come back. I'm ready to create meaning."

As I walked, I passed by a woman wearing a scarf on her obviously bald head. Her eyelashes were missing, and her eyebrows were penciled in. I caught myself staring. *Fuck, that's how people probably feel when they look at me. They catch themselves staring with pity.* Then, it hit me: what if I used my October retreat as a cancer survivor's retreat in my mom's honor? I was badass at hosting fundraisers (a.k.a. parties), and I could fundraise the $6,000 it would take to bring a group down. I had already put down the deposits for the Ensenada hotel, anyway; no one had booked yet.

But something started stirring in me; that anger began to turn into fuel. Newton's law was repeating in the back of my head: "Energy cannot be created or destroyed, only transformed." I could feel my helplessness transforming, the helpless anger suddenly gaining a little bit of purpose. It was addicting.

When I get an idea, I tend to roll with it at fast speeds, and this was no exception. I started Facebooking and reaching out to every single one of my connections from my internship at Susan G. Komen, and basically told them that I was having a free healing retreat weekend for any survivors.

But who would trust me? I've never had cancer! Who am I to know how to host twenty survivors? I just had a mom that died. I turned around to look at the woman walking away with the headscarf, and some tiny voice told me it would be okay. I knew what it felt like to have to shed an old identity and start a new one; we shared in our visible disability. We shared the same plight to create meaning in a shitty situation. We shared the same pain of fear, the unknown, and having to face a new normal. If I was going to be stuck this way, I had to live for something bigger than myself. I couldn't be the victim; it didn't look good on my badass, boss-bitch persona. I also would not now, nor ever be, a tragic optimist. So, I would be in service to my meaning and immediately got to work on my "What's Next After Cancer Healing Weekend" itinerary.

The retreat sold out in five short hours. I mean, it was free, but it still felt so good, knowing that there was something there. I was needed, and the survivors were so appreciative. They didn't know me or my story, and it was amazing to know I could start fresh with them. I know when survivors get a "clean bill of health," they are left with a physical appearance that was hardly recognizable to their past self. Like my mom, they were left with no eyebrows, no hair, no eyelashes, lots of injuries, and a bloated shell of who they used to be. They wouldn't stare at me funny, because they understood.

Later that night, I shut up my inner critic and emailed Amelie back, nervously accepting the Lululemon cover model shoot. Confidence is beautiful: my butt wasn't paralyzed, and I could still hold a damn handstand. The German girl came back to me, saying, "Don't let anyone ever tell you what beautiful is."

My three-day outline was pretty simple: "Show Up, Give Up, Align Up." We "showed up" together by playing ice breakers and volunteering at a local orphanage to get out of our heads and into our hearts. On the second day, I helped participants "give up" limiting beliefs and break through old thought patterns. Those days are always the deepest and darkest, so I bookended it with a wine tour through Valle De Guadalupe to shake off any of that shadow work.

The first two days went as predicted with my Cancer Warriors group. They had fun with the orphans and expressed such deep gratitude for the experience. Cancer or not, it's hard not to be grateful for your life when you see a Mexican orphanage. Your heart melts, and you want to do something bigger for them and for the world. On the second day, the inner demons came out; as humans (and apparently cancer survivors as well), we all experience the same suffering. We want love, we want our bodies to look better in some way, we want health, we want certainty, we want significance...we want self-respect.

The third and final day is typically the most fun for my participants and me. It's the day that we dream "Oprah big." I help them "align up" to clarity in their calling. We uncover passions and goals and make tiny steps towards their dreams. We act out, improv-style, some of our wildest dreams coming true, toasting champagne and giggling at how ridiculous we looked.

Having hosted this itinerary dozens of times, I felt pretty confident in the material. But day three with my Cancer Warriors completely rocked me, especially after peeking down at my journal entry from my last retreat in June. We had filled in the statements, "When my life is ideal, I am..." with ten butterflies-in-the-stomach-scary statements. In my seminars and workshops before Bell's palsy, I would normally read things like, "Continue to teach at Wanderlust around the world...Become a global ambassador for Lululemon...Teach for YogaGlo online...Teach at the International Yoga Festival in India...Have three kids with Matt...Have enough money to take my entire family on vacation." The list went on.

That day with my cancer survivors, my dreams felt different with Bell's palsy. Recently, I'd been so day-by-day, focusing on just trying to survive, and praying that my face would heal. It's easy to dream big when things are going right; it's not so easy to care about "taking my whole family on vacation" when my fucking face doesn't work.

I heard one of the women let out a whimper.

"I can't do this exercise," she said, bursting out into open sobs. I waited patiently for the sobs to subside so that she could continue. "I have no idea how to look forward. I've spent the last year thinking I was going to die; I don't know how to look past today. I was scared that I was going to die for so long, that I've lost the ability to dream."

I know the feeling, I thought, looking down at my own notebook. *And I'm not even faced with death. I'm just faced with a broken face.*

I took a deep breath before speaking.

"I don't know how you can regain your ability to dream; honestly, it's taken me a while to do the same thing myself. I just know that since we get to breathe today while so many others don't, I like to believe that life is happening for me. This exercise is one that asks you to think about the future so that you can be hopeful in a sometimes-hopeless world.

"I want you to fantasize a little, like you did when you were a kid. Before the world told you who to be and weighed your courage down with negative experiences. And once you've done that, you'll realize that life happens *from* you and *for* you.

The world isn't the way that others see it; it's the way that I see it. I want to help us all change this fear of the future into something fun to look forward to. So, Christy, just start small and build a dream for two weeks from now. What would your ideal life look like in fourteen days?"

She sobbed again, and this time, the whole group quieted down to listen and support.

"I think," she sniffled, "I'd be doing a daily walk, playing with my cat, and sleeping through the night."

"That's perfect," I smiled, encouraging her. "Now let's go bigger. Did any of that give you butterflies or make you nervous to say out loud?"

She paused, truly searching.

"No."

"Then let's think about upgrading your dreams by going bigger. You feel strong enough to do a daily run, not just a walk. Your cat finds another cat whose owner is smoking hot and thinks you're amazing, too. You gain a new cat friend that could maybe turn into something more. And you sleep so soundly that after a solid eight hours of rest, you wake up naturally without an alarm."

She was shaking her head "yes," but her head was so buried in my arms at this point that I could only feel it. What a coincidence; I was smiling, but because of my paralysis, it was hard to see. However, I knew that she could feel it. *Make them feel your smile, Katie.*

Our closing ceremony was a receiving line. The Cancer Warriors made a tunnel, and each person, eyes closed, walked down the line slowly to receive a whisper from each of the other participants. It's one of my least favorite exercises. *Why is it so hard to hear how good you are?* I especially didn't feel good this year and was dreading the slow walk. However, I took a deep breath, crossed my arms across my heart, and started to walk down. Their hands guided me gently, and each person would pause at my shoulder, lean in, and have their moment to whisper. With my eyes closed, it was so much easier to hear and receive.

"Katie, I can't thank you enough for this. I am so thankful that you took something tragic in your life, allowed it to give you purpose, and that WE were able to RECEIVE it. I am forever changed."

Angel bumps rose up on my arms and legs, causing my hair to stand up on the back of my neck. I kept gently walking down the line.

"Thank you all for making me laugh and cry so hard this weekend; my heart is full. I know your mama is so proud of you."

I started to ugly cry. It's hard not to with Bell's palsy. It's hard not to when my mom is brought up. The inner ache of missing her churned in my belly; I wanted her here more than I'd wanted anything else in my life. It was a deep and familiar feeling.

"Katie, I think this whole cancer journey had made my inner wild child pretty pent-up. Thank you for letting her hang with you Saturday night. Ooooh, tequila; how I've missed it."

I started to laugh through my ugly cries and kept walking.

"I don't have the words, Katie. You showed me that yoga was more than moving. You showed me that I could actually move again. You showed me it's okay to open up." She started to cry on my neck. *"I hope you understand what you've given us. I can see forward for the first time in months. I have a little hope. I'm not as scared of the world with the new me, bald or not."*

I turned and gave her a full hug, the kind that moms give their daughters, the kind that I had missed out on for so many years. *Yeah, I was helping these people. But, just like everything else I've ever done, it started selfishly motivated. I needed this. I needed to know I had a purpose that wasn't skin deep. Fuck, what a beautiful gift I was given, that I created out of thin air. I did this. Life happens for me (I guess, thanks Bell's palsy and mom dying?), but also **through** me.* You see, I had given my anger forward momentum and transformed it into good; that first Cancer Warriors retreat will always stay with me. That happened because I took something bad and made something good.

As the week of the Beverly Hills photo shoot approached, I was still very paralyzed. I wasn't fully happy, but I still felt fulfilled with a purpose. I had regained confidence in my swagger that I had lost at Wanderlust, and through my Cancer Survivors retreat, finally found it again.

And then...*it happened.* The tiniest thing that meant the world: one microscopic nerve twitch, one flicker of hope—*my eyebrow moved!* I had been recording myself every day to see if I was missing any new movement and would show it to Matthew later. Today, just short of three months in, I got an eyebrow twitch. Research said that if you got any movement back, it meant that you'd probably get most of it back. I'd been waiting for a day when there was any movement, so I screamed from the bathroom and called Matthew immediately. *I can't believe it. I got it back. It's coming back! Thank you, Mom; thank you, Universe...thank you. It's coming back.*

It's easier to think life is happening for you when it's working the way you want it to. And boy was I celebrating the Universe with that simple eyebrow movement. It turned into a full eyebrow lift. On the day I was driving up to Beverly Hills for the shoot, my eyelid was closing mostly on its own. I could wear my contacts again, as long as I kept the eye drops coming. My smile lifted about 50 percent.

Never having done a real modeling gig before, I was cray-cray nervous when I pulled up to that Beverly Hills home. I had to yoga-flow my way through the new Spring 2016 collection outfit changes to keep calm, and the entire crew raved about my strength. Carmilla, the make-up artist, wowed at my arm balances. Gary, the director, applauded how long I could hold challenging postures. Shannon, the hairstylist, laughed about how in their Asian promotional markets, they would probably have to photoshop out my badass tattoos. We had the best day, and they never once asked about my face.

At the end of the shoot, I said to the entire crew, "Did you know I have Bell's palsy?" Gary stopped putting his camera away and glanced up. Carmilla looked over in silent disbelief.

"In August, I woke up with the entire right side of my face paralyzed." The room went quiet. "I couldn't blink, smile, or hold food in my mouth. I couldn't say F, B, or P sounds. It's been slowly coming back; I'm at about 50 percent now."

I recognized the familiar, funky looks they had: they were sizing up the sides of my face. It's like one of those games where you have to find "What in this photo does not belong? What is different in this photo from the other?"

"I didn't know if you guys knew," I continued. "I thought that maybe it was a driving force behind me getting the gig."

"No, sweetie," Carmilla laughed as she continued cleaning up her makeup kits. "We had no clue. But it obviously didn't matter."

Gary walked over and put his hand supportively on my back. "That must have been hard. I'm so sorry."

"I'm doing my best to work with what the world gave me, not against it. I don't have it figured out in the slightest, but I do know that it feels better to believe the world is working for me than to doubt it. I'm trying to write this chapter of my life as a good one, even though it's been fucking awful. If I have to force good things on myself, I will. Life happens through me. I'm trying to be a hero in my own goddamn story. I'm trying to be the person I believed I could be when I was a kid. And the days that fear wins, tequila helps."

He laughed at that last bit.

"Can we celebrate with tequila on days that are good, too?"

"Done. But only if it's none of that José Cuervo nonsense."

"I know just the place. Let's go create some meaning, eh?"

NAMA-CRAY CALL TO ACTION

5. Life happens *for* and *from* you. You can't control what happens, but you can control the meaning you give to it.

   A. Bow to the experience: there's a strength that grows from your story. You dictate the meaning. What part of your life can you create meaning around?

   B. Bow to the shitty parts of life: they make good stories. How you tell your story is how the world will remember you. What narrative are you writing about your life?

CHAPTER 6

Bow to Your GPS—Puffy Eyed and Powerful

"It's going to be sunny; Mom always pulls through!" I said, flashing my beautiful pearly whites. Amy and Becky, a power-couple-bestie-duo of mine, had flown all the way from San Diego to meet my family. Matthew was in the front seat chatting it up with my dad, and my two best friends were sitting squished with me in our old family Jeep. I felt a little jealous that Matthew was so fun and light with my dad. *Why is Jim Burke easier to laugh with than I am? What am I missing?*

This is the trip I'd been waiting for. The sticky, humidity-filled Friday was so damp that your skin had a layer of dew immediately after leaving the air conditioning. Amy and Becky had both grown up as West Coast kids. I mean, they asked for a real Jersey experience, and they got it. This was annual-summer-trip, hair-curling, inner-thigh-chafing, back-sweating, hard-to-breathe kind of weather. It had been three years since my Bell's palsy diagnosis, three years of living with Matthew, and three years of a new normal for me. But why did it feel so daunting? My insecurity center was on high alert; I was on constant defense, unable to shake the feeling that I would either lose something I wanted or find out something that I didn't.

"What happens if the Seventeenth Annual 'Kathy's Tube for the Cause' is rained out?" Amy asked, genuinely concerned as she looked at the deep gray skies.

"It's never been canceled; Mom always pulls through. It's always sunny," I said again, far too matter-of-factly. That notion kept me afloat each year, even when it rained all week leading up to the event. *Yes, I can control the weather. Or, at least, my fear. Mom's on the job; she can do something for me even after she's passed.*

"She's right," my dad, Mayor Jim Burke, chimed in from the front. There he went, always my number-one support system. God, I love that man. He takes all my fears away. He fixes all.

Amy was an old boss and mentor turned lifelong friend. She'd taught me everything I knew about hosting personal-training-style boot camps. I only had four short days to show Amy and Becky the craziness of my Guido Jersey family in the place where I grew up. They've known me the older half of my life. My yoga life. My Lululemon-wearing, constantly sweating, hyper-motivating, healthy, and active life. Now, I got to take Amy back to what I'd call my "emotional boot camp." Going home always made me turn into that same stupid teenage girl who lost her mom: reactive and ungrounded. The same boozy bitch who drank Southern Comfort while driving her mom's old Subaru through the country roads of Queenstown. I'd always said that going back to New Jersey for a few weeks would be the best emotional boot camp I'd ever gone through. No matter how many times I tried, I couldn't seem to bring my "Guru Katie" back to Jersey. I drink too much, get mouthy, and say mean things to my stepmom and anyone else who gets in my way.

I'd see my mom's three sisters hosting family Spaghetti Sundays without her, and I'd lose it. I'd run from it. You'd think being three years out from my Bell's palsy diagnosis, I'd have a better state of compassion, but no. I lose any semblance of empathy when I go home. The little hormonal Beezy fires up and loves whiskey-infused oversharing. Nevertheless, I was determined to do better this time. Matthew has always been an excellent buffer for my exaggerated emotional states with my family. He's the comic relief I need, my hammock, my safety net. He's my manly muscle when I'm about to step (or stumble) over the line.

It was a perfect Family Friday at the pool. The rain had cleared enough, encouraging the kids to swim in the thick summer heat. Between Guido toddlers' joy-filled screams, WJJZ smooth rock radio in the background, and the high-pitched conversations between my mom's sisters, we were in full Jersey Summer swing.

I sipped my Coors Light and gratefully scanned the scene. Amy was laughing it up with the kids in the pool. Becky was gabbing away with my aunts about the tomato pies and my family recipe for the pasta sauce. Matthew was tanning shirtless with my Uncle Dick and talking golf between sips of Heineken.

I remember saying, "Take a mental picture." I remember asking myself never to forget this moment. I applied my cherry Carmex on my lips to keep them shiny, taking a grateful moment in with a big, bright, fully operational smile.

I almost forgot I ever had Bell's palsy. I almost forgot that my mom was missing. I almost forgot that Uncle Dick's eyes tear up whenever he sees me, because he misses my mom so much. I almost forgot last month's conversation with Matthew about him moving solo to Los Angeles for school. I almost forgot about his college, where he got accepted for his master's in art therapy, and how it lost its accreditation last week. I almost forgot the look on his face when the goal he had been working towards, the saving grace of our relationship, called and told him they were shutting his dream down, and he was left back at ground zero.

I looked at him, laughing with Uncle Dick, and was reminded that family is so fucking nostalgic. It's so hard. Add some Coors Light and a few secret shots of Don Julio, and my emotions will start talking louder than my mind. Family reminds you of what was, and in your goddamn memory, the grass was always greener. They also tease you about what could be: the hope and potential are endless.

I saw Matthew's hairy chest dripping in the Jersey humidity. He kept flicking his dreads back and re-tying his bun to get those heavy locks off his back. *God, I love you, Matt. I have enough love for both of us and for what we've worked for. I can see us. I can see it so clearly. Matt, can't you imagine our cute Italian Lebanese kids with curly afros and tanned skin running around in diapers giggling?*

Don't you remember that time in your kitchen, right before I had Bell's, when you said to me, "I can't wait to look back on this moment at the end of our lives and say, 'Remember when you used to come over to my studio apartment and I made you dinner? That little studio with only one chair, so that you had to eat in my lap?'"

You dreamed about the end with me—you saw us old and gray. But I know something's wrong. Why are you thinking of ending it sooner than we promised? Sooner than I dreamed? Our families go out to eat together. Our grandmothers know each other. It's always made sense. We are a love story for the ages.

My inner self clung so hard to this moment. I didn't want it to end. Matt "cheers-ing" my uncle, laughing with a big bold laugh. He must have felt my clinginess, because he looked over, with a half-interested, passive-aggressive smirk, and lifted his beer to mine. He was pulling away. He wanted me to break up with him first, because he wasn't capable of facing his gut.

The following morning, as promised, Kathy came through for us and brought the sunshine. What we didn't ask for was the several days of rain leading up to the Tubing event, which made the river dangerously high and fast. What would have normally taken four hours to ride down now took less than one hour. The speeds were so high that the owner of the tubing company decided to ride along next to our group in his boat just in case. Everyone was mandated life vests, and no kids under eighteen were allowed.

You could feel the fear building during the pregame in the parking lot. My friends, who had traveled at least two hours to get here, took a few extra swigs of Faderade to shake off their fear of embarking down the Delaware River rapids.

I got up onto my dad's Jeep, in my giant pink Crocs and Kathy's tube hat, and started my thank you speech.

"You guys know that I live in beautiful San Diego. When I get home, around my family, around my mom's six siblings, I get wrapped up in the 'what ifs.' Yesterday, I had a spiral moment, looking out at the rain and asking for Mom's help. I thought to myself, 'What if I didn't have to do this every year? What if Mom was still around leading the family tubing event, and not me?'

"I think that this is our plight in life: to cherish the moments we do have, without getting lost in the 'shoulda, woulda, coulda.' To be brave enough to celebrate the breaths that we do have, and to take them in honor of those who can't.

"That's what today is to me, my brother, Patrick, and my dad. A celebration of Mom, and a promise to ourselves to move through the life we have left with a brave and open heart.

"I can guarantee that I would have had to work really hard to convince my mom to go to a yoga retreat," I laughed. "That's the irony of what we're supporting. But I want you to know that we're supporting something magical with your donations today. Here's some words from last year's survivors."

I pulled out my phone and started to read: "'As a five-year survivor of breast cancer, Katie's retreat was exactly what I needed. Once I got through the treatments and surgeries, everyone just assumed my journey was over, but I still had the emotional aftermath to deal with. I was able to meet women who knew exactly how I was feeling, and I made friends I will love and cherish for the rest of my life. I cannot thank Katie enough for such an honest, raw, emotional, fun-filled experience.'" I put my phone away and smiled out at the crowd.

"I hope you guys understand that Mom is felt in all of the people we've helped so far. Mom is here laughing with us now, and ready to drink a beer and pee with us at the same time. Thank you so much for showing up."

The crowd erupted in cheers. I set the microphone down and waddled off the top of the car, my Crocs making a *squeegee* sound against the hood. With our life jackets secured and Faderade (vodka in Gatorade bottles) filled bellies, we started to walk towards the water. Suddenly, several State Troopers pulled up with their sirens on, stopping us in our tracks.

"We can't let you get in this river."

"Come on, guys," my brother bargained with them. "We're good swimmers. We were just going to tube for an hour in my mom's memory."

"I'm sorry," the Trooper said. "It's too dangerous." As soon as he finished that statement, a twenty-foot tree, with roots as wide as its height, whizzed past us in the river. An empty, capsized canoe followed in its wake.

I looked at our group, apologetic. "I guess the silver lining here is that we can go back to the hotel and party at the pool.

At least the sun is out. I'll issue a refund to anyone who wants their forty dollars back. I'm really sorry, guys; this is the first time in seventeen years that this has happened."

My heart sank as the dozens of people decked out in pink *everything* started streaming back to their cars. Becky and Amy had flown all the way from San Diego. Patrick had friends that had flown across the country for this moment, only for it not even to happen.

I felt myself losing all control. I couldn't fight the State Troopers. I couldn't make this better for Amy and Becky. I couldn't give back the countless hours it took for the 200 people to get here this early on a beautiful, sunny Saturday morning. But what I *could* do was throw a damn good party. For the fifty or so people who opted to party with us at the hotel pool instead, we took over that dinky Radisson like we were at a fucking wedding.

I bought shots for everyone and made sure everyone felt seen. I thanked them countless times, and once the fifth tequila kicked in, I repeated my gratitude like Dory from *Finding Nemo* by drunkenly hugging everyone. I drank beer, floated in the pool, and peed in the pool with my people, and from what I remember, I loved it.

Matthew didn't.

I kept applying my cherry Carmex, that stupid, fucking Carmex.

I loved the way it made my lips look. The right amount of shine-like gloss, the right amount of cherry to make me smell sweet, and just the right amount of "Chapstick" to not be too girly. I knew he didn't like that fucking Carmex; he'd told me multiple times. Was it about control? *Why would I put something on my lips that he said he didn't want to kiss?*

My gut knew something that my heart didn't want to know. The drinking lately helped my gut quiet down, enabling me to cling to the notion that Matthew and I were okay. Every time I took a tequila shot, every time I applied Carmex, every time I was loud, I was pushing him away subconsciously, not wanting to admit what I already knew. Between his school getting its accreditation taken away, his inability to tell anyone at my family event (with his entire family there, too) what he was doing next, and my Jersey girl drinking coming out, this particular Saturday was a recipe for our disaster.

In a world where we have no control, one thing we can know for sure is the end result of repeating old patterns. I knew that if I blacked out, I would get the end result of pissing off Matthew, me not remembering, and everyone else having a fun time. So, I chose the known. It felt better than the constant unease stirring in my gut that was unsure of what Matthew was thinking.

I blacked out at some point that night, but I didn't care. Someone donated an Adderall pill at some point to my cause, and the rest of the night is straight Nama-cray. Or so I heard. Becky, Amy, and the rest of my crew seemed to think it was funny the next day while I ignored Matthew and his condescending looks. *At least I could control that outcome; my world as I knew it was unraveling. Matthew was something I counted on. Was I blind this whole time?*

Being the yogi badasses they are, Becky and Amy vowed to come back so that they could actually tube, but they, like everyone else, let me keep the donations. The silver lining was that instead of giving the tubing place $20 per head, we could make twice the amount and bring eight more people on a healing weekend for cancer survivors. I had to keep holding on to the silver lining. *What was going right, Katie? Focus on that. Look past, drink past, move past everything that doesn't feel right. There's always a silver lining, right?*

The week we got back, Matthew had promised me that we could go have dinner with a British couple that had started "super-fanning" in my class. Originally from Ghana, Orion had the most amazing stories to tell, and he and his wife had moved here to start a church following Jesus. They were so emphatic about me and my message that I wanted to see a part of their life more intimately.

In the three years since my Bell's, Matthew and I created a beautiful little beach home, complete with a driveway, an old neighbor, and even a bird named Puffy that lived on our porch.

Living with him felt easy; I loved coming home to my man because he felt like home. Decorating walls around us just felt normal and easy.

Only two nights after our big tubing trip, Matthew dragged his feet the entire five-block walk over to Orion's house. Our hands sweated as we held each other, but the sweat gave him an excuse to pull away from the hold casually. *How did we go from walking arm in arm as equals, no...skipping arm in arm, to me dragging him? Is this how our life was going to be? Him always trying to side-step and walk on in the street while I'm on the side-walk? Where was my knight in shining armor who saved me from myself during Bell's? Where was my home?*

The sun was still bright at six forty-five in the evening when we came to their two-bedroom apartment. Once we walked in, Matthew was perfectly normal, his kindness sexy, and his smile endearing. He genuinely loves meeting people and getting to know them, so I suppose he'd been saving his tantrums and passive-aggressiveness only for me lately. *How lucky.*

James, the oldest of their kids, came up at seven and asked if they could go to bed. I was incredulous; I had never seen children ask if they could go to bed. Pastor Papa Orion asked if they would stay up just a little longer to hang out with their guests, Matthew and Katie. The four-year-old and two-year-old stared up at James for their collective answer.

"Okayyyy," James said with a bit of a six-year-old sigh.

We've always been good at playing with kids; I don't mean to brag, but I'm most definitely a kid whisperer. They remind me of where we came from. They're the closest things to "God" or the Universe that I've ever seen. They're so present. So brave. Unadulterated giggles. I've never felt more connected to God than when I stare into an infant's eyes or hear a two-year-old giggle. Man, could these kids giggle, and Matthew was the best at bringing it out of them. Kids loved to jump on his shoulders, as if the width mirrored a jungle gym's stability.

When the kids went to bed, our two couples sat and gabbed as we told our origin stories. Orion and his wife, Ericka, were awestruck by our physical beauty. At first, I felt like they were trying to recruit us for a foursome because of the way he so deeply complimented our physicality. He'd say things like, "You'd make beautiful babies," and "Wow, you are both just stunning creatures," in his British accent.

As we shared our love story of the ages, Orion and Ericka brought out a scrapbook of theirs. What a fun book filled with stories of their nineteen-year-old DJ escapades and their mutual love of Jesus Christ. I loved it. They're so fucking interesting.

Matthew played along with the love-story telling. He divulged how he'd cleaned my yoga room for months before I noticed him, how we stumbled home together and I fell off the bed taking my shirt off, how for seven months of distance, the Universe still managed to bring us together in Chicago and Argentina; how all those stories were meant to be. For a split second, I even forgot his passive-aggressiveness on the walk over. It felt so good to remember that love, and I marinated in every second of his stories.

When the night was over, we quietly walked home, arm in arm, and fell asleep in our giant Cali-king bed.

I'll never forget the way the sun hit his skin the next morning. We had tan blinds that let in too much light in the morning time; he loved waking up with the sun. I didn't.

We started the day the same way we had for the past three years, by saying three things that we were immediately grateful for. His felt fake. Mine were forced but joyful. I kept searching for what was going right. *I know us. I know our potential. I know you, Matthew. Keep believing.*

The avocado-sized pit in my stomach had been rotting brown since last week. My heart was finally strong enough to take the chance.

"Matt," I rolled over on my left bicep to look at him.

"What?" he said, still staring at our stucco ceiling.

"I want that."

"What do you mean?" He was already losing patience.

"I want what Orion and Ericka have. I want three little rascals that we've created. I want them to be so close and so awesome they put themselves to bed while it's still sunny out in the summer! I want that love, that unit."

He took a deep breath, and I could see a tear welling up in his eye.

"And I don't."

My tears were a sideways waterfall dripping down my face. Laying underneath our covers in fetal pose and staring at the love of my life, I said to him, "So you have to have the bravery to say it."

"I know."

"Then say it. You have to."

"I want to break up," he said slowly and carefully. It was actually the sweetest he'd spoken to me in months. "I'm lost. I can't find myself in you anymore. I thought I could, but I can't."

Uncontrollable tears flooded my pillow, and snot dripped out of my nose like a spigot. His tears fell down his temples, past his big ears, and into his dreadlocks. I buried my head into my pillow and sobbed.

"All this work. All this time," I started to say. "What about your grandmother? My grandmother? Nan was going to give me her ring. I'm her favorite. Don't do this, Matthew. Don't do this."

He rolled to his left, away from me, and sobbed even harder than I was. His animalistic sobs were guttural and so deep that they stopped my own tears. My instinct wanted to hold him. *Fuck you. I want to hold you. Fuck you for leaving me. Fuck you for giving up. Fuck you for being a fucking pansy.*

We took turns sobbing. We held each other, sobbed, stared into space, and sobbed again. He finally got up out of bed, and I texted a friend to sub my morning class. *SOS. My heart is broken. My heart has been fucking lying to me. It's been blinding me. My gut has been telling me something, but my heart has been louder. Fuck you, broken heart; I can't teach class.*

I can't even remember the rest of that day. I blacked out in emotional anguish and just faked getting through it like a robot. I knew it was real. I knew he was gone. The next night, we just sat on the couch together and snuggled. We comforted each other in pain we both caused one another. I couldn't not be around him, but I didn't want to be near him. My clingy, crazy bitch was at level ten, but I didn't know how to move forward without him. My safety net, my hammock, my home, was gone. He did it. He fucking gave up.

We were both confused by still loving each other but not being in love. So, we just sat on that tan couch. The worn slanted pillows were uncomfortable, but we didn't care. My leg was over his lap, and my head nuzzled into his strong jawline and clavicle. The August heat without air conditioning made our skin slick together, but I couldn't let go. Just like the Bell's, I couldn't bear the thought of telling the hundreds of people I see each week what happened. We were a poster couple. We were a love story for the fucking ages.

"Do you think I can post something, babe?" I asked him.

Should I still call him babe? It felt so wrong. Am I allowed? Someone else is going to call him babe...holy shit. I held onto his arm tighter. His ugly nineties corduroy pants that he loved so much felt hot under my inner thigh. My tears stained his old yellow tie-dye shirt. His hair was like Albert Einstein's, sticking up high out of his head. I started to kiss his neck.

A part of me flashed back to the first time he kissed me with a broken face. Where his tears literally dripped into my stuck open mouth as we tried to figure out how to navigate the new normal the world offered us. But we navigated that *together. I can't do this alone. I don't want to do this without you, Matthew.*

We started passionately kissing, the kind of kissing that started that fiery tequila-filled night when he walked me home. The night I fell off the bed while taking my shirt off. The night I thought I'd found my fucking soulmate.

He threw me down and rolled on top of me in the masculine and sexy way I'd been begging him to for the past year. He dominated me. I felt all of him. The tears turned into passionate thrusting. I felt like I was floating, being held by his arms, his body, and his heart. This was what making love felt like.

I could feel our energies being transformed: the stuck energy from our hearts, the months of his passive-aggression, the months of my partying to forget, all of the couples counseling sessions, his feelings of insignificance in my thriving business, his lack of direction when his school called...it was all being pounded out with each thrust and biting kiss. I felt my heart scream, *I need you.* Not the need of a life partner—the need of a lover. I needed every part of him right then to show up, because I knew it would be the last time.

When we finished, breathing so heavily, we cried. I felt so much worse and decided to start writing to get it all out. Once I'd composed a way to tell my friends, family, and followers that we were splitting up, I took a deliciously puffy-eyed selfie of us on our couch. I posted:

Heartache Chronicles—Chronicles of heartache: my sweet

Matthew. This photo, we are even loving after a good ugly cry together. It's so hard. We see different futures. In this breakup, I've learned the difference between my gut and my heart. My heart wants to stay in his arms. Like I have been the past five-plus years. My gut knows he needs to fly in a different direction and because I love him so much...insanely actually...we have to separate.

Sometimes, two good people can't take the same path forward. So, I sit and let it flow out of me.

We met when he was cleaning the Pacific Beach Inner-SteadyYoga. I saw this sexy, Johnny Depp kinda guy, and he made it religiously to my Tuesday eight o'clock in the evening class. After a fateful date (Tabu actually came out to approve) and some dancing (fueled by tequila), we were inseparable. God, almost six years. I lose my shit thinking of the work we've put in...years of self-work on ourselves and our relationship... and our families.

Yet, I have faith in this man and know that if he needs to fly, he will find what makes him soar. Even though it kills me it can't be me. We have a choice in despair. We can let the snowball of thoughts roll into WHAT IF/WHY/SHOULD HAVES, or we can sit in the thick of the emotions, feel them.

Let them flow through us and have faith that there's a reason undiscoverable to us right now. That the magic dance of the

Universe eventually provides. Thank you to those who have supported us throughout the years. —*Love, Katie and Matthew*

I felt like, in some way, I had taken the narrative back. Realistically, he had broken up with me and it was ultimately his choice to give up. I was still ready to fight. But deep down, I didn't realize that the real fight was between my heart and my gut until we actually broke up.

There I was, yoga master extraordinaire. A boss bitch with my own 501(c)3, a solid yoga following, and I had overcome facial paralysis. And all I did this past year was run from the one thing I consistently preached for my students to tune in and listen to.

"Namaste" is a traditional greeting in Hindi that is commonly used to say *hello* and *goodbye* in India. "Nama" means "I bow to the light," the light that's inside us. I call it the "Guidance Powered Source," or GPS system. Ever since I watched my mom's light die out with that last fucking exhale, I'd been supposedly bowing and seeking my light for years. But here I was, doing everything I could *not* to listen. I hadn't known until that moment that my gut and my heart weren't saying the same things. My heart wanted so badly to stay, but my gut was a tiny whisper, tugging on my coattail, telling me to let go. It's so easy to suppress it. It's not loud. It's not a fucking billboard. It's small. It's waiting for you to listen.

Matthew knew what he was doing; the timing was just right.

Compounded with the school losing its accreditation, he knew that I'd be leaving for my normal three-week stint in Europe for one of my company's hosting trips. He had eight days before I left. We broke into pieces, and then I left for Ibiza.

August 18, I left a day earlier than the crew that would meet me out there to go over logistics. I texted my assistant/little sister/best friend from the Barcelona airport, "I should have had you come with me. I'm a mess. I'm so alone."

I knew that the Mediterranean and its music could heal. I was surviving through the day, not thriving. I was just trying to make it breath by breath. I kept sitting at the depths of my personal Rock Bottom Cafe, which ironically was the Ibiza airport, the entry point into European summer euphoria, where people go to get high. The first day alone with the leaders, you could find me secretly crying in my pillowcase, Insta-stalking Matthew, secretly hoping that he would post something. I had flown as far and as fancy as I could away from my life, and I still felt fucking rotten. I was puffy eyed at least 50 percent of the day; I had nowhere to go. I had to sit in it. No tequila, no dancing, and no remote bougie island were going to take away this feeling. So, on arguably one of the world's most beautiful islands, I just sat in it.

The more times we visit the Rock Bottom Café, the easier it gets sitting on its disgusting, tear-soaked sofa chair. It feels more reflective, like, "Here I am again...What did I do this time? What can I learn from myself this time?" As sad as I was, I felt like this breakup (compared to my earlier ones) was easier. This is not creating lifetime wounds; it's just tearing muscle. Your adversity is your advantage. Let your scars become your super-powers. *Blah Blah. I hear it. I just can't feel it yet. And so, it flows. And so, I sit in it. Fuck you, time. I know you heal all wounds, so hurry it up.*

Even though being the retreat leader kept me distracted, I still felt daily stabs in my heart and gut. It was his sister-in-law's birthday. *Fuck me. I can't believe we're not going to have babies together.* I really wanted a sister. I wanted a mother. I wanted what we created.

All I remember is what it felt like to move my body to the beat of David Guetta, the final summer set of Martin Garrix, Calvin Harris's closing set at Pasha, and the sea of people wanting to lose themselves in the vibration of that island. I took our group to sunset ashram, and as we sat watching that yellow ball of fire say goodnight, I remembered that it was my mom's birthday. August 29, so removed from the world, I came back to a familiar sense of the calendar with just enough time to say goodbye to the sun. I cried as it set, cheersed her with the crew, and then clapped like an Asian family when a plane landed. I posted:

Life is often a series of waves. I sit out and watch the sunset over the beautiful Mediterranean Sea in Ibiza. So grateful that

I'm breathing. I've been happily distracted for at least ten days. Meeting new people, having new experiences. And sometimes the world is crashing down on you with the empathetic depth of the human condition. We are literally just one drop in a giant ocean. It's like we are just a cup of water pulled out of the ocean, and then we leave this body and are dropped back in. The body of water is never any different.

Happy birthday, Mom. Your life is just a cup of water taken out of the ocean. Upon first glance, one cup doesn't make a difference. But it's the multiplicity of cups added together that makes the vast ocean. When we leave the body, the cup is put back in that ocean of energy. Better because we return back home. We can spend all of our days in fear and anxiety and worry about things that may or may not happen in the future. Or we can rep the muscle of trust. Trusting with an open heart that there's a purpose in our being here in this body, in the time we get on the earth. I sit watching the Ibiza sunset grateful, a little broken. But definitely hopeful.

I had the unique pleasure of hosting three back-to-back weeks of retreats, which meant I connected with fifty-six humans. The final week, I was in my favorite happy place: Sardinia, Italy. Each week got further away from the feeling of him but closer to the anger I felt about not valuing or listening to my gut.

Saltwater heals. As the days passed, and my skin soaked in that healing liquid, I detached just enough from him to see a glimpse of myself again. My solar-powered happiness allowed me to see hope amid my emotional agony. I knew, although unforeseeable at times, that there would be an end to this stabbing pain. In the same way that I had initially missed my mom with insatiable need, that hurt eventually dulled to a tiny tremor. Time is a motherfucker. It also motherfucking heals. I hate when old euphemisms are right. So, I sat in it, posting again:

Nineteen days away from home. I can't tell you the wave of emotions I've experienced from being away that long. I've cried as many days as I've laughed. I danced and partied to put a wall up to forget.

My heart goes from tears of sincere gratitude...a life I've worked to create...and then quick tears of worry and regret.

Fuck.

How can the world be so insanely, randomly beautiful, and then feel like the world is crashing down ten seconds later?

I am living my dream life. Traveling the world, meeting new amazing people, seeing this vast, expansive world.

And in that vastness, there are still moments of emptiness. Moments where I can feel like the smallest ant. I am so grateful for these moments. It reminds me I'm alive. Receiving the nectar of what life has to feed me. Learning from the heart and the gut.

I am open. Are you?

Falling will happen more than rising, so what if our real goal here on earth is to be graceful in the descent? To stand so radically in our sense of self that when the outside world collapses in, we can withstand the weight of the fall?

Sun-kissed and salty-soaked skin, I could start the long road to healing and forgiving myself. My inner light was always there; I had just chosen to ignore it. It was time. That familiar feeling of knowing that it was time to say hello to my spirit again. I had to turn my own volume up louder.

I sobbed every day. But still, I had to be in service to my self-love more than the love I so desperately ached for from Matthew. Through the tear-stained days, I understood that I had to be more focused on where I was headed than who was coming with me. *But fucking fuck, it hurt.* I was at a tipping point where muting and numbing my intuition was more sickening than sitting in the reality of being dumped. In the cycles of our human experience, there I was again, getting to know my new self for the first time. I was ready to listen.

6. It's a constant journey of knowing yourself. Your inner GPS is always guiding...if you dare to listen.

   A. Bow to your inner GPS, even when it fucking hurts: it will always guide you if you're willing to hear it. What are you avoiding?

   B. Bow to your inner GPS: it's always guiding, but sometimes, you forget to turn the volume up. Be in service to your self-love—love yourself the way you wanted them to love you. Where can you love yourself more audaciously?

CHAPTER 7

Bow to the "Single B." Chronicles

Becoming newly single makes a woman in her thirties *insanely* horny, and I mean, *loco*. It's like I suddenly understood the puberty hormones of a fourteen-year-old boy and how sex could dictate choices so deeply. How does a person go from consistent sex in a relationship to nothing? The fact that it wasn't just in my bed and available whenever made the craving even more insatiable. In the first sweet months of singledom, I got very acquainted with my own body and the many fantasies that I'd wanted to play out. But, for me, something was missing without that partner. Being held makes my nipples hard. Being admired makes me wet with appreciation. Just the thought of a deeply shared love can make me orgasm without any physical contact.

My new normal was a prescription of tequila weekends, plenty of time spent in half pigeon, a lot more hands-on assists than before to get my physical touch dopamine boost, and flirting with old flings. *I know time heals, but why is this taking so fucking long? Newsflash, Katie: no one's coming to save you.*

I'll never forget the moment that I began to shift, almost half a year after the breakup.

Every night for the past few months, my normal M.O. was to get home, see "our bed," and miss him. The clouds of white pillows that I'd concocted as a pseudo-boyfriend were equally comforting and heart-swallowing, because they served as a silent reminder that he wasn't in it. It had been a landing pad for so many nights of passion. Lately, I'd been drenching myself in those goose-feathered throw pillows, swallowed up by the need to feel held, spooned, and kissed by his stubble on my neck. I missed the way his chest would rise and fall, the subtle comfort of knowing that he was there, even if just our toes barely tickled together. Every night, I'd miss his musk, the kind that stays after someone's been in your bed. I'll never know if it's leftover morning breath drooled on the pillow, back of the neck sweat, or just a general pheromone sensation...but I'd still miss it. I missed everything.

But this particular January night, I giggled as I landed in bed with my glasses on and retainers in, looking my sexiest ever. I had that coy, flirty grin on my face that you only get when you're texting a love interest. Something was different. I didn't notice the emptiness. I didn't miss his smell. I could almost barely remember it. I gasped. *I don't miss him. Holy fuck.*

I started to cry, realizing that I was forgetting what it felt like to love him. What it felt like to feel loved by him. I couldn't forget; he was so good. We were so good. *But were we? Katie, are you doing that reasoning-and-excuses thing you've always done for him?*

Time was doing what it should—heal. And yet, I cried because I knew that as my heart calloused and moved on, I'd forget him, too.

I still have this journal that I kept when my mom died that contains the small details about her...like how she had a blue vein dot on her lip, or the way she kept her nails just a fraction of a centimeter with white and short enough to look clean. Or the way she smelled like Dove soap, but fuck, I couldn't remember mixed with what...you see, I had forgotten her. I didn't want to forget him, too. I didn't want to forget what it felt like to love him.

I had giggled at first, loving my alone bedtime for the first time in years, and then cried, because I knew the inevitable was happening. I was forgetting what it felt like to love and be loved by him, and it was finally time to move on.

* * *

His name was literally Richard Dickerson. Fourteen months after Matthew gave up, I decided to jump into the deep, unknown world of dating apps. The story I'd been telling myself was that dating apps were just for needy people and way too difficult to find a good person on. *Come on, Katie. The past is a place to learn from, not live in. Be excited for the chance to look inward. Growth is so sexy.* So, I decided to take back my description of dating. I had noticed that I'd been replaying the story of what others had told me about online dating, instead of experiencing it for myself. Dick Dickerson just happened to be the first. The tacos sucked at the beach bar we met at, but it turns out that he did not.

We were in the same place, mentally and emotionally. We were light and teased with a sort of East Coast sarcasm. He was so in sync with my humor: funny, quick-witted, and with the smile of a fucking rock star, this midwestern boy came with more than just height.

I felt awkward meeting a twenty-eight-year-old as a thirty-two-year-old, but man, I felt young and small the minute I met him. My alpha-female demeanor had no chance looking into his boyish hazel eyes a good foot and a half above mine. He was part of something in the military that I didn't fully understand, and it was sexy. Our first night of getting to know each other felt like my first night with Matthew: we giggled, we were playful, and it was easy.

Cheap, soggy, fish tacos on a weird Thursday Halloween night led to meeting up with his military friends at a local bar to dance. We were flirtatious the entire night, and he looked so damn sexy. I hadn't had sex in weeks. Maybe months. Maybe I was so blinded by my throbbing celibacy that while we were still at the bar, I texted him, *"Hey, this is fun and all, but I'd rather hang with you solo? Lol."*

In the past year, I'd fooled around with friends where there had always been sexual tension between us in the past, but I hadn't actually dated any of them. If this guy was what dating was like, I was in—totally smitten. As we walked, Richard put his big hand on the small of my back, as if to guide me. He looked at me like I was the best prize he'd ever won. What I saw in his eyes from this silly date was the initial date validation I needed to keep going. I knew that I was the only person capable of coming to save me, but damn, did it feel good to be admired. We ended up back in my giant Cali King bed, which I had lovingly started to call "the cloud." He had been teasing me leading up to this moment with his charm. His size matched his strength, and he threw me around in ways that I'd always wished Matthew did.

He was only visiting San Diego for the weekend, which made it perfect for me to lust-love him, knowing that there were no strings attached. This made his coming over around ten o'clock in the evening after work on Friday night, and in some casual sweats, not weird at all. I loved the fact that there was a boy who wanted to just hang and have sex with me. The fact that my roommate, Liz, was gone helped, too. She'd said encouragingly, "Have sex everywhere," and I intended to let Dick Dickerson carry me all over the house. Having two names that mean "penis" is hard to live up to, but he rose to the occasion, and then some. Again, and *again*.

Saturday kept the infatuation going, with us sharing weird videos with each other of our past and encouraging secret inside jokes after just a short thirty-six hours of knowing each other. We continued to joke about surfer gangs in Australia that he didn't believe were real, and the crazy co-birding we'd done two nights before together on a scooter. His size made it challenging for a scooter to power both of us, making it hilarious to go uphill. The deadline of his return to Arkansas validated our too-fast, lustful love.

Sweet DD had some night operation drills that kept him from the Saturday Halloween party I'd attended, but he met me later at my house around two o'clock in the morning. A part of me doubted that he was telling the truth about "night drills" with the sergeant, but whenever he came into my room, I made sure that my sex lights were on and low. I pretended to be asleep, rolled on my side, giddy with excitement that he was finally there. He pulled my ankles, opening my legs so wide and so hard that I slid right to the edge of the bed, my pelvis meeting with his instantaneously. I was so wet with anticipation of him. He ripped my underwear off (I literally only wear them if I know that someone will rip them off) and showed me so much love that I came just as quickly as he put his face down there.

He's thrusting, he's kissing, and it's insanely powerful. I am all in. He's deep in. He picks his head up from our make-out session, and a trickle of ocean water pours from his nose. The salty spew drenched my face as I laughed in utter hysterics.

"I'm so sorry," he said apologetically. "When I dive, water sometimes gets lodged so far up there that it hibernates and decides to drop out on its own."

I was laughing so hard that I couldn't contain myself, covered in seawater from his nose. I guess he was telling the truth; look at me, growing in more ways than I can imagine.

I can't contain him. He falls out as I roll over, laughing on my level. The laughter created a new level of intimacy. That was one of the weirdest things to ever spew on me during sex, and we still were so hot for each other.

When we finished, he asked me, "What did you like? What can I do better? I want to know what makes you feel good so I can keep doing it to you. You are one of the most beautiful creatures I've ever seen." As if I wasn't already gushing literally and figuratively, I needed this pure admiration. We spent two more nights together ravishing each other's bodies.

I wanted Dick Dickerson to walk in the door and surprise me at Tuesday night yoga. I cried when he didn't. I stood at that door waiting for some Cinderella-style surprise like Matthew would have done. I wanted the beginning of this to be like the lust-love Matthew and I shared. But, as all men do, he told me what the situation was. He was leaving back for Arkansas, so what we'd had was just weekend fun. The issue was that my newly-single-bitch heart didn't know how to handle liking someone again only for it to end. I didn't have much practice in this. It was all so new.

I don't want to do this all over again. My heart ached. I don't want to go up and down and up and down emotionally only to know that there's inevitable heartbreak coming. *No one's coming to save you, Katie. Stay focused on where you're going, not who's coming with you.*

The girls started to fly in that night for our teacher training trip to Mexico. As my Boston crew arrived, I came in teary-eyed and spilled the DD story. They sat like little kids listening to a teacher read at story time, wide-eyed and curious about my lust-love.

"If all dates are going to be this intense, I can't do this," I cried. "It hurts like I'm losing Matthew again. I really like this kid, even though I know it won't work."

The parting texts weren't what I wanted to hear, but there was clarity in his shortness. I had my answer. It wasn't the one I wanted, but I had it. Since the breakup, whenever I felt a "maybe" in my gut, I knew it was a NO. Whether the "maybe" feeling was coming from a guy and his response to me, or me getting that feeling about someone else, I knew I had to take every maybe as a "no." *You know deep down what "yesses" feel like.* I wasn't his yes. If there were one girl-power chant that I could paint on every billboard or show on every newsfeed, it would be this: "MAYBE IS ALWAYS A NO."

Deep down, I knew that he wasn't my yes, either. I just wanted to keep playing out the fantasy that dating was really this easy: the first guy I met on Hinge was actually my damn soulmate? Too good to be true! I took a deep breath and took back my power in the next text.

"Thanks for reminding me how much fun I am, Dick Dickerson." And it was done.

I needed to end it with something that validated the independent woman I knew that I was. *Where is the fine line between independence and being a fun, vulnerable, loving girl?* With his clear response, a familiar guarded feeling bubbled to the surface. Anger came to the forefront of my mind. It's so hard to put yourself out there and take a risk. You have to like yourself A LOT to take a shot. I don't know if my self-worth was high enough post-breakup to handle liking someone and being "rejected." It's so hard, as a human, to be honest with people and speak your truth, because there's a huge chance they're going to say something that you don't want to hear. There's always the chance for that. *So, is it still worth it? Why can't I crave my own adoration, instead of his? Why do we get so lost in competing for their admiration that we forget to ask ourselves if we even like them in the first place?*

Matthew had always shown me who he was. He had always said he didn't know if he wanted kids, never said he wanted to get married, and would hold back when I started talking future *anything*. He was comfortable at his level of "drive" and felt too pushed by mine. Yet, I was so willing to hold onto the vision of who we could be that I neglected to see what he was. I was in love with his potential and not his reality. *Why do women's minds travel so much further into the fake future? What will it take for us to be goddamn present and just enjoy life?*

That year post-breakup had been a whirlwind of healing and drunken escapades. I wasn't just upset at Matthew for giving up—I was pissed at myself for not listening to my own gut. For the entire last year of our relationship, I had been making compromises with both my intuition and the Universe. I'd ignore a sign or signal they sent via the relationship, but then, I'd just go deeper into helping cancer survivors. I'd make sub-conscious mental compromises, hoping that the guttural tug to leave Matthew would go away if only I fundraised more money for my orphans in India. I'd reason that every relationship has its ups and downs, and this season would pass.

I couldn't believe how I'd short-changed myself, and a lot of my healing was forgiving myself for not listening to myself. I felt betrayed: not just by him but by my own excuses.

About a year out, I immediately hit up a long-time crush named Brian, who was never available or accessible when I was single. I'd been waiting for years to lick his eight-pack and get lost in his hairy, delicious man bod. When I was angry with Matthew during our relationship, I'd text Brian, "How's NYC?" and harmlessly fantasize about getting my mental revenge. He was always the "sexy one that got away," who was harmless to text and feel loved by when Matthew couldn't give it to me.

He came down for a primal weekend, and we wrestled and rolled all over my beach bungalow. It was so fun to have sex with a longtime friend, and the orgasms were that much better from a fantasy boy I had written off since I'd been so invested in making Matthew my everything. Brian was my first "life pop quiz" to see if I could listen to reality, instead of making it morph into what I wanted it to.

He was perfectly fun. After two weekends of pleasure, I could feel a part of me wanted to see what could be more. I'd tease a few phrases here and there, like, "When are you moving back to San Diego?" He didn't bite, and his answers were basic. He wasn't mean; I'd just not been in the dating world for years and didn't know how to read his answers.

The first red flags were his inability to spoon and disinterest in cuddling, but I had written them off. His dad-like goofiness and bright blue eyes were amazing enough to make excuses for *a lot*. This Greek stallion had only been in one "barely-there" relationship, and even if he were signaling that he liked me, neither one of us would be able to read or send the right signals to meet each other where we were. That was clue enough that I shouldn't push it; we were in vastly different places. *No more falling in love with potential. Keep on your quest of self-inquiry, Katie. Let's be obsessed with our own potential for a change, eh?*

The needy, scared part of me had wanted him to say, "You're my dream girl. I can't wait to move to San Diego to be with you." I could feel that familiar stirring of a magnetic clinginess brewing. It's a scary feeling, like I was losing control of my self-gratification. Like I was handing my happiness over to this sexy fucker after only two weekends of fun. *If no one is coming to save me (and I know this logically), then why does one compliment via text message light up my day so deeply? No, Katie. Don't you dare read into something basic.* This is a young, relationally-inexperienced man. He's showing you exactly who he is, just like the men before him. They don't have six different layers behind everything they say; that's why you like them. *Don't fall in love with potential. Believe patterns, not words.*

Although I was still angry at myself for ignoring my gut towards the end of things with Matthew, I couldn't add to any more regret. How did I let myself get so disconnected from myself? I would do anything for that fucker. I held my friends and family to such a high standard, and I let Matthew get away with so much more. I made excuses for what I thought at the time was him, but if I'm really fucking honest, I was making excuses for my inability to take a chance on something uncomfortable. Happiness at 70 percent was better than the uncertainty of singledom at thirty-one. This whole time, I'd thought that I was protecting him and us, when I was just protecting my own god-damn self and hiding from a deeper truth that I wasn't ready for.

I cried a bit in frustration but knew the truth: I didn't think that sweet Brian was my person, either. I just wanted it to be that easy. *Nothing worth having is gained without a lesson of struggle, Katie. Focus on loving yourself the way you wanted them to love you.*

My fling with Brian sparked a beautiful streak of rendezvous with long-lusted guy friends, and even an old girlfriend. A random bartender in Malaysia, a photographer in Italy, and some of the sexiest people I'd ever hooked up with. My new normal was crying at least once a day, scared shitless of not having a "home" in Matthew, fearful of not having kids, and ashamed I felt lonely. I spent many solitary nights surrounding myself with my seven pillows, attempting to make my bed feel not so lonely...yet somehow, I still managed to find my own sexuality. This was a time for me to figure out what it was to love myself again, in all the right ways.

I embraced being both happy and hurting at the same time,

which I had never been able to do before...the ability to hold two true emotions at the same time. I'd cry myself to sleep with loneliness only to wake up with tears of gratitude, thankful that I was free of the weight of hanging on...the endless feeling of loving someone more than they loved me. *Fighting your gut is fucking exhausting.*

It's time. I've gotta look forward despite the swirling past withdrawals. I have to be more addicted to my growth than to my comfort. I have to stay more focused on the places that I'm headed than on who's not coming with me.

But where the fuck do I want to go? Time to start trying new things with the intent of learning more about my cray-cray self.

NAMA-CRAY CALL TO ACTION

7. **True, lasting happiness is a practice of constant growth. Fall in love with the process of self-inquiry and you'll have a love affair with yourself that never ends.**

    A. Bow to your journey of growth: true happiness is the conditioning of discovery and growth. Bow to the life-long adventure you get to have with the coolest person you know, yourself. Where can you turn your lens of focus to growth?

    B. Bow to your inner cray: that's what makes the journey so damn interesting. True self-worth can only be quantified through your own description of success.

CHAPTER 8

Bow to the New You—Fuck the Q

Sitting alone on my couch, with no one to care if I eat one cheddar Nut Thin or 400, I stare down at my yellow-stained fingertips. No one is telling me to watch only one episode or to binge forty hours straight (*yes, Netflix, I'm still fucking watching*). I feel like I'm on a never-ending snow day.

We've got the official word from the world that life as we know it is canceled. Spring 2020 is just straight-up canceled, and the buses aren't coming to pick us up. Quarantine 2020 has started, and the highs are so high, and the lows are so goddamn low.

There's this giddy, freeing vacation mindset that makes us feel like we can eat all the things and watch all the things and drink all the things. But as the weeks have passed, the fun, snow-day vacation mindset has shifted to jail-cell mentality. The fast-paced life I've created has come to an extreme, exponential halt. As fun as pretend-life has been—with late, beer-pong-style nights at the house because it didn't matter what time I woke up, let alone care what day it is—it was getting increasingly lonely.

Sitting here, with my belly hanging out over my yoga pants and eating my second box of Nut Thins, I feel stuck. Stuck in the same way that when the snow gets too thick, you have to stay inside. As the snow piles up, inch by inch, you realize that snow days are only fun until you can't get out to see your friends, and sometimes, the fucking power goes out. Well, my power has gone out. It's not fun anymore.

When I know that I have a date to look forward to over the weekend, I get excited to eat clean, work out hard, and pick out something sexy and fun to wear. There is no COVID dating for me, though. I have so many Zoom clients keeping me busy that I've refused to try to connect sexually through a screen for now. So, my solo nights have been filled with very eclectic homemade dips and "New Girl" reruns, getting lost in someone else's romantic drama for a change.

Fuck you, 2020. I was just starting to find my dating groove, I think. Didn't you see my 2019? Dating isn't so bad once you've got a few under your belt. I wasn't totally happy, but I was less uncomfortable, and I'll take that as a win any day.

Life is just a series of mini conditioning opportunities to make your heart and head stronger, and COVID was proving to be a series of unwanted opportunities for mental and emotional growth. I always say, "You either are growing, or you're dead." *Or maybe I stole that from Tony Robbins. Who knows?* I chose to take these opportunities to foster growth, for the most part. Messy, sticky, ugly, awkward growth. Normally, I prided myself on being so busy improving my life that I didn't have time to criticize others, and when things got difficult, I'd take a shot of tequila and try again the next day. But now, my world was getting smaller and smaller each day. I was actually making my bed and caring about cleaning my curtains. *Who am I?*

In pre-COVID January, about eighteen months after the breakup, I took one shot of tequila before the date instead of three now (*#winning*). I enjoyed my time getting to know these random Hinge guys, and at the same time, I enjoyed being seen. It took me so long to build up the self-love again to risk the rejection. I was finally almost there (with the help of less tequila).

I even got to four dates with one guy, and he asked me to be exclusive. The shock of his long and articulate text made me realize that I wasn't dating with an open heart: I was dating to practice dating, not to meet someone. I was shaken right down to my cold, callused heart. *Am I so broken that I can't see the way back to love? Ouch. Less tequila next time? Or maybe more?*

Arriving home after three back-to-back trips to Mexico, Nicaragua, and India with my teacher-trainers and yogis, I told myself that I was ready to open my heart to dating and to find my next human...my next soulmate. Someone that could reflect my awesomeness. Someone with whom I could see my truth even clearer. I was ready to be seen.

And then, the Q(uarantine). Fuck the Q. The Universe's way of pretty much saying, "Close up, Katie; close shop, and shut up." I found myself putting emotional and mental Band-Aids on every facet of my life. That snow-day mentality was strong.

Owning an international retreat business that operated off a steady stream of deposits for upcoming bi-monthly trips made my finances take an interesting turn. I found myself in debt for the first time in years. Coupled with my brand being dependent on my in-person classes and networking with students, COVID was rocking my skills and financial identity.

I, like most cool trainers, started dating Zoom like it was my soulmate. I put a mental Band-Aid on everything I'd built. But month after month, as trip after trip got postponed, my heart sunk deeper. No in-person classes were coming back anytime soon and definitely no international trips.

My spiritual practice went from being so completely open to guarded and shut down completely. At first, I worshiped COVID, like it was this universal enemy that didn't discriminate against race, color, religion, country, or beliefs. It united us with a common veneration of our healthcare and service workers on the front lines. But, as it always seems to do, bi-partisan US politics loomed its ugly shadow and infected a separation on even the most globally uniting force, a fucking pandemic. I started getting quieter in my opinions. And risks? Ha, non-existent. Why would I take a risk when everything was already crumbling? I was in survival mode. Go inward, get quiet, and hold on to the last pieces of myself I could.

I bandaged my relationships by forming an "igloo" family of six of my single friends in the initial two months we were quarantined in San Diego. In that time, I would have been leading a teacher training in London, attending a wedding in Israel, surprising my friend at the finish line of the Boston Marathon, and leading a group of thirty people to Sayulita over Cinco De Mayo. My first-world traveler's heart was broken, and any semblance of connection was severed into survival mode.

My social interactions became Sunday nights sharing cheers with Dwayne "The Rock" Johnson as he took shots of tequila on Instagram live, attending the *Some Good News* "Prom" fully dressed in my prom dress, and doing Zoom beer pong with my now online clients and boot campers.

When April got really hot at the beaches in San Diego, we started a weekend "truck pool" by filling up the back of our friend's truck with a tarp and my hose. We made a fake "bar hop" around each room of the house, played strip variations of "Cheers to the Governor" where we used pillows as belts, perfected the TikTok game, and lost track of time in twenty-four-hour benders that made me feel like I was seventeen again.

Snow-day mentality felt like a vacation mindset: I could get away with so much. But at the same time, I felt stuck. I broke two vibrators and probably went through an entire twenty-four pack of batteries in the initial weeks, but just like any momentary happiness, it fleeted. *Yay, I can masturbate eight times today, but shit, I have no potential to put a warm body and some intimacy behind those orgasms.*

Quarantine with COVID-19 has been life's way of shoving the illusion of control right in our faces. We go through life as if we have some semblance of control over what happens next, because our human perception can't handle the fact that we absolutely don't. We could stroke out at any moment, but if we kept living in that state of mind, we'd paralyze ourselves with fear.

As we locked up and masked up, I felt my heart locking up and my smile disappearing. Any ounce of single-girl sensuality was masked just like my lips. I craved affection and attention in the ways Brian and Dick Dickerson and my Italian men had given me. The art of kissing and playing was long lost, and I was starting to feel like a shriveled and dry cat lady, minus the quarantine cat. *Even all the fucking animals were adopted; no dopamine hits for me. I am truly losing it.*

No matter how many Zoom cheers or workouts with friends I did on Facetime, this quarantine rut tested my mental capability of knowing myself and feeling whole. It had been asking me to figure out, in the face of a new normal, what makes me *me*, when my normal things are stripped away. My retreat business was my spiritual reset. Traveling was my identity. My students were my family. Teaching was my favorite part about me. And now, all I had was my living room and my ten-block radius. I am a firm believer that your direction is more important than your speed, but *how on earth could I find direction locked in my living room?*

By August, I was spiraling. Every reset button I had in my pre-COVID identity was lost. I didn't have my 600 students a week to work through my own problems out loud. Teaching was my therapy. *But wait, did I have problems if nothing was going on? Did overeating Nut Thins and watching too much TV count as problems? Champagne problems aren't real, right?*

I didn't have my own practice. I didn't have travel to reset my small-mindedness. I haven't had a deep kiss or touch in months. I had so many emotions and nowhere to express them, so I started writing letters to my emotions.

Dear giggle-faced old Katie,

I miss you. I remember when you used to love loving. Remember how good it felt to nuzzle in your partner's arms? Remember how much you loved feeling safe? Like it was home? Come back to me. It's safe to trust again. The world has shut down, but your dating world doesn't have to. Look for opportunities to meet people on your walks. Stay open.

I know...shhh...it's hard to fall backward and watch your heart shatter. You keep finding a way, but it's so fucking hard to piece it back together only to know that it'll be broken again. Love threads everything together in life. You have to fight to get it back. Come back, my giggly, loving, sweet Katie. I don't know where you are. You had a nice tequila-infused vacation. It's okay to try again. Don't give up. The world's full of second chances.

Scared shitless,

Your safe, independent self

The letters made me feel like I had a secret friend within myself. They made me feel a little more balanced in a world where I had lost all of my normal tools to rebalance.

Dear Boss Bitch,

It's okay to own this new online Zoom venture. It's not what you wanted, but it's what you're getting. You're ready. The world has been waiting for you. You have to be willing to hear a "no" from the people that you don't want to (the wrong people) so that the people who are actually looking for you can find you (the right people). Just keep taking a step forward. You don't have to have it all figured out.

Don't look back. Just jump. Five, four, three, two, one...prove it. There's a trampoline at the bottom if you fall. You'll toe touch and bounce your way back up. There are too many people cheering for you behind the scenes.

Emphatically,

Quarantine, Non-Risk-Taker Katie

Somehow, writing these letters became an outlet for all the fucked-up things I was feeling. In August, during round six of my virtual online boot camp, I basically told them that the magic I used to feel was gone. And I had to say it out loud so that it could get off my spiraling mind. I had to figure out a way to create my own luck again and look for miracles in new places; I just couldn't find the motivation. *Seriously? I'm a goddamn motivational speaker and an amazing coach, and I still couldn't find it*. So, I took back my own words. In theory, I can understand them, but emotionally, they feel so far-fetched.

I know that purpose gives us power and meaning as humans, so I had to rewrite the "woe is me" narrative that I'd been spinning. It felt so fucking fake, but I decided to speak my new life into existence. I took back the narrative by taking each mundane moment and making it into some sort of small fucking miracle. In reality, they're not some divine sparks. Most of the time, it's me just closing my eyes and chanting "One, two, three...go!" and not looking back at the critical thought spiral.

That Thursday in Bootcamp, I was out in my driveway with forty or so boot campers on a Zoom call, sitting in my bikini and getting my tan on, not feeling the slightest bit sexy. In Jersey, we have that slogan, "If you can't tone it, tan it." Well, watch my tan hide my insecurities. This particular August Thursday, I may have had enough of my own shit.

I told them, "Team, I am so not myself. I'm saying this out loud to proclaim it so I can change it. I know balance isn't found—it's created. But I'm not creating it right now. I'm completely out of whack and can't find my reset button.

"So, there's a hot guy across the street who works out with his kettlebells in front of my driveway every day. Before Sunday, I am going to walk across the street and introduce myself to this hot "kettlebell" guy and be brave. I don't feel sexy. I don't feel myself. But I have to do it." I finished, extremely uncomfortable.

"Katie!" Steph, the hot-mom boot camper unmutes herself. "I'm going to stay on the Zoom with you right now until you do it!" My tan skin turns to beet red at the thought. He was right there. His sweaty, beautiful body was cleaning and jerking that seventy-pound kettlebell like it was a baby toy. He looked like a Brazilian Jiu Jitsu fighter.

"Steph, I promise by Sunday. I can't right now. But I promise by Sunday," I finished, full of butterflies. I stared down at my bikini body and sat up straight to suck in insecurity.

I set an end date to my personal dare, and I meant it. I could feel the energetic shift. I was proclaiming to myself and the world *I'm back*. I'm ready to be seen. Even if it's 49 percent fake. Watch out, kettlebell guy. I didn't suddenly feel sexier. I just decided to stop telling the story that I wasn't ready. *Time to create your own fucking luck, Katie.*

Not fifteen minutes later, as if dropped out of a fucking rom-com script, a sexy, sweaty, shirtless, green-eyed man jogged the long thirty feet up my driveway to introduce himself to me at my patio table. A DIFFERENT hot neighbor, who'd been running past my driveway for months gaining the courage to ask me to work out with him, literally waltzed up my driveway minutes after I proclaimed to the boot campers my rock bottom.

"Hey, I'm your neighbor, Robert. I see you working out here every day. I live a couple of houses down. We should work out together."

I looked over at my assistant Michelle sitting at the table with me. I was incredulous, almost speechless. If only he could have known what that moment meant to me. I don't even care who he is; that was the Universe telling me *fuck yes*. You're back in this. The Universe was giggling, "You give a little hope, Katie, and I'll run with you in that direction."

His sexy soccer legs ran over as promised the next day to work out, and it ended up being the first workout date I've ever had. On top of that, it was also the first SOBER date I'd ever had. I found myself actually intrigued by this guy with high white workout socks and a voice so deep I swore he was faking it.

With his incredibly talented, athletic background, Robert was about as opposite as the dreadlocked artist Matthew as they come. Robert didn't want to contemplate universal paradigms with me, but goddamn was he honest, assertive, and simple. I needed simple. In this adorable and admirable simplicity, I needed to shelter him from the crazy things I was feeling. I needed this hot, Italian Jewish man to be easy. He didn't need to know how bruised or broken and cray-cray I am. But he sparked something in me I couldn't hold in. So the daily balance letters I had been writing slowly shifted towards him, without him ever reading them.

Dear Driveway Boy,

What about that particular day made you run up my driveway? That thirty-foot walk to my front patio table felt a lot farther on that Thursday afternoon. Did you see the pure shock in my eyes? Followed by pure admiration in your goddamn COVID bravery. Did you know I was asking the world to be brave myself that day?

Did you know that just minutes before, I told my boot campers that I would go ask out a different hot guy across the street who works out with his kettlebells? I was feeling super disconnected and not myself. COVID was getting to me. I'd gotten so used to keeping to myself I'd started to forget my old, risky, sexy self. And then you waltzed up the driveway so confidently. To shock my loud mouth into silent awe is already a good first step.

And Friday, woah. I didn't expect to see you. That's why no one was there but me and you. Especially not less than twenty-four hours after you approached me to work out together. You actually did what you said you were going to do? I'm in awe of your actions. I miss that bravery in myself.

It was so awkwardly perfect. I've never had a workout date. I think it was a date? Yeah. It was a date.

Your one-legged deadlifts were wobbly, and I didn't know how much to coach you or not. I was actually nervous. You caught me so off guard two days in a row that I was giddy in confusion. What a fun specimen you are.

I'm so glad I got to stare at the Zoom screen and work out with you rather than coaching you. When I caught a quick gaze, I saw your green eyes glimmer, and I blushed. Who are you, silly neighbor boy? How long had you been running past me? Why that day? What do you have to teach me? What more ways are you going to shock me?

In appreciation,

Your nervous boot camp "coach"

By proclaiming I was going to change my story that day in August, something shifted. The bravery that "driveway boy" showed that day was the exact reminder I needed to reignite my post-quarantine self.

Quarantine has made a lot of us lose so much. For me, there was an unlearning of how to socialize with audacity. Having not been SEEN in a few months by fresh eyes and an open heart, I was fucking scared to be seen. And yet, that story needed to shift. I was the only one who could create that balance for myself. No one else can.

So that Friday night, post-workout date, when I said yes to a late-night Bud Light, when Robert leaned in to kiss me, I leaned in, too. Contrary to the Universe dropping him in my driveway, it wasn't some rom-com first kiss. Our nervous lips kind of missed, and then gently found their way back together. I was squirming in the awkwardness of the first kiss, and at the same time, squirming with glee because it was all still okay. There's that weird pause where you don't know if you should go back in, lean left or right, kiss harder or softer, until we found the balanced dance. I was ready. After months of hiding, I had to try something. This didn't feel easy, but it was sparking a part of me that was excited. That was enough.

Whatever that new and simple love affair was becoming, I didn't care. I was so out of balance at this point, I was just happy to know the butterflies in my stomach still worked. It was a reminder that I could feel again after two years of trying to rebuild a self-numbing hard edge to stand in my power.

But you see, here's the thing. Because I was open to the shift, and brave enough to say yes to asking "kettlebell boy" out, even against my better judgment, the world opened another door. I didn't feel 100 percent ready to ask him out; I barely felt 65 percent ready. But I decided to make a shift. I created my own luck, without the guarantee of success, because I had nothing to lose.

Robert sparked a flame in me that had been flickering close to death. I remembered what it was like to love a part of me again. I remembered what it felt like to love the butterflies again. I was proud of myself. That part of me that was also insanely brave, like driveway boy. Driveway boy isn't the savior; my reflection of my own bravery, stoked by his example, is. I was chasing myself again, not necessarily love. I found the spark to recommit to discovering my balance.

The key to lasting happiness and balance in life isn't finding love or family or abundant money or travel. It's finding meaning and purpose in a life that's always going to rock you. The only constant thing is change, and it's the quest for purpose and meaning every day in the little things that makes it worth it for me. Change is inevitable, progress is not.

Life sucks, a lot. If we understand this, then every day is a practice of finding your own balance and definition of success. You see, that Thursday in August wasn't a one-time thing. The raging doubt and insecurity will keep coming up. Life will keep bringing me back to the proverbial Rock Bottom Cafe. But what if my soulmate is sitting at the bar and asks me out down there? I can live as if everything in life has meaning or as if nothing does. Creating meaning in all of the drunken blackout nights AND the magical driveway boys, now that's balance. My balance is mine to explore every day.

I wrote this poem, which I lovingly titled, "You Are Made of Magical Shit," to sum up my inner-forced revolution. Repeat it out loud if it serves you. I walked my neighborhood for days chanting this to myself in the depths of my isolation.

We all feel a little lost sometimes;
We've all BEEN at a loss sometimes.
When you feel that hole starting to open,
That gaping emptiness widening,
Get quiet and ask yourself...
What is the shortest distance to my depths?
And what does my inner GPS system want me to know?
It's easy to forget
To save some of you, for you
It's easy to forget how to relight your spark,
When your inner shadows make it too
     dark to see the way out.
Let this prayer be the exit pathway to light your way home—
Thank you to all my embarrassing moments,
Especially to those I can't even remember.
I've learned how to validate myself
     instead of outside approval,
Unapologetically fierce in the pursuit
     of my own empowerment.
I'm ready to create magical shit.
I am ready to throw up confetti in the back of life's Uber.
I'm saving my fucks for things that light my soul on fire.
I am a broken badass that takes shots of life's magic.

8. Bow to the New You and Fuck the Q. Balance isn't found; it's created.

    A. Bow to the shedding of old ways: the only way through is forward, and it doesn't matter who comes with you. Where can you just take one step today that makes you proud?

    B. Bow to the work: the messy, gooey, hard work. Luck is the residue of your design. You're in the driver's seat, so where can you take back control?

Conclusion

How do you throw up confetti in the back of life's Uber if there are barely any Ubers running? How do I still feel magical when this chaotic world that we live in is so predictably unpredictable? Our human minds lie to us, computing that we have a high probability of the same consistent thing happening each day, when in reality, we could get hit by a bus any moment. The consistent factor here in this world is instability.

Figuring out who we are in that instability is the way to freedom, and every day is a constant practice of leaving space for the "cray." If I overbook my schedule with arbitrary things, I'll have no space to rock with the boat when it sways. If I move from checkmark to checkmark on my to-do list, I'll barely look up enough to see that the world is shifting, and creation is at play. If I set up too many Hinge dates, I'll leave no space for spontaneity and the randomness of meeting my next human in the driveway. If I resolve that masks block my sensuality and that six feet of separation guards love's body language, then I've already lost any chance of adventurous romance.

I, like most humans, gravitate to old dramas, and even more so in quarantine. Because so many things are unknown, old issues feel good because of their goddamn familiarity. It's easy to fall back into the rerun of your own fucked-up mental foreplay. It's easy to get lost in your own tunnel of regret and self-sabotage. At least you know how that one ends. I've tried being reinspired by my old ways, and it's not working. No tequila dancing, trips, new flings, or Ted Talks can get me there. It's time to recommit to myself, and to the luck that I want to create in this life. Nothing worth working for right now will feel easy, and you're going to have to condition your mental commitment to yourself every single day. But guess what? The world is waiting for you to love the new you: *do you have the strength to find the new post-2020 version of yourself?*

The pandemic has taught us to ask ourselves that, although we are unseen in some ways right now, when the quarantine veil has lifted, who will we be? What do we have to offer this world? Have I made myself essential? You have to be a conscious choice-maker now more than ever, so start asking yourself, "What do I have to offer?" Our society has been drowning in information but starving for wisdom: we have been plagued with 'intention deficit disorder.' People have been coming into each day as carriers of fear instead of love, panic instead of patience, and status instead of empathy. It's time to look outside of our broken selves and add to the light within others.

The breaking down of this world has enabled us to break up with bad habits and break free of old beliefs. My search for meaning, despite years and years defined by my mom's death and my Bell's palsy, has only just begun again. Our post-traumatic growth now makes me ask, "How am I essential in this new world? How am I in service to love and my best self?" As my happiness has severely faded in COVID, my search for meaning has only gotten stronger. I want a new relationship with everything in my life—Nut Thins and alcohol included.

It's kind of ironic that all this happened in 2020, don't you think? Twenty-twenty vision is the clearest. What if this was some giant, cosmic joke that we are actually now clearer in life than we've ever been before? I guess it works if you define clarity as knowing the people we want to see, being more loving to those we get to see, becoming more resilient in the weird shit we go through, and growing more human.

Remember, there's a reason that you, out of the 120 billion people who have died on this earth, are still breathing. It's not a mistake that you woke up today, and each day is an invitation to figure out why we did. You have to be yourself, and you have to keep owning who you are, because how else are the people looking for this new post-2020 you going to find you?

What if everything you're going through right now is preparing you for something bigger than you've ever dreamed? What if everything has meaning, and we just have to take it and create it? What if you spin it in your favor by not seeing things as they are, but as *you* are? The biggest flex is loving yourself the way you wished everyone else did, so be your own damn upgrade. Be who you needed when you were younger. And it takes being loyal to your future, not your past, to get there.

Most of the time, it's me faking the funk until I know it to be true to who I am. Most of the time, I'm faking it until I make it, repeating something better that feels foreign until it becomes a pattern and habit of who I am.

I know from experience at rock bottom that it works, at least most of the time. When it doesn't, however, there's always tequila, a vibrator, and another chance to inhale, bow to your crazy, and wake up to try again tomorrow.

Here's my anthem: when you need an energetic reboot, when your inner critic is louder than it needs to be, or even when you just need a reminder to live today like it's one of your last, read this out loud with fire. No...*scream* it out loud: the world is waiting to hear you!

I bow to my humanity and my inner crazy: if I'm honest with it, it never leads me astray.

I bow to the moment: it's fleeting.

I take responsibility for my intimacy with this moment. I won't get it back. It's mine for the loving.

I bow to my fear: my vulnerability is my pathway to real connection.

I honor the shame, guilt, jealousy, anger, confusion, blame, insecurity, and sadness in me as my window to love.

Negativity arises to remind me of the places I've forgotten how to love.

I bow to trust and faith: good inevitability rises when I seek it out.

I know I have the courage to see what's going right instead of what's going wrong. I am a lighthouse shining an example of how I live, not a life raft to save and Band-Aid.

Life is happening for me, not to me. And life happens through me and the lens I choose to view the world.

I bow to the breakdown: breakthroughs come.

I know it's who I am in the downfall rather than the rise back up. I trust the times I fail, inevitably more than the times I'll succeed. I vow to be better at failing and enjoy the lessons it provides.

I bow to each experience: I know my strength grows from how I tell this story.

I know I can't stop the experiences that come, but I can control the meaning I provide. I'll write the narrative in my favor.

I bow to my inner GPS: I'll turn the volume up as loud as I can.

I vow to listen, even when my ego gets in the way. My life is a cultivation and a practice of hearing that voice and guidance.

I bow to my practice of being a human: I'll commit to the practice of grace within the growth.

I commit to the practice of growing, no matter what form it drops in. Happiness comes from conditioning gratitude, grace, giving, and growth.

I bow to my journey of creating balance every day.

I know that balance shifts. People change, the world changes, time passes, and the only thing I can control is my reaction to it all. If I create my own balance, the world can only rock me, not knock me off my feet. I create my luck.

I bow to my humanity.

I bow to this human experience.

I bow to my inner cray.

Just In Case You Need the Reminder

Honor the beautiful crazy in you. All the answers you need are within you. I am not teaching you anything new. It's about reminding you what you've always known, but life experience helped you forget. Bow to the cray.

NAMA-CRAY CALL TO ACTION

1. Change is the only thing that's constant; your circumstances can shift in an instant. The here and now is a gift, not a given, so treasure it.

   A. Bow to your intimacy with the moment: it's fleeting. Can you recognize that you won't get it back? Everything dies, and everything ends. The only thing that's certain is fucking uncertainty. How can you honor the moments you have today?

B. Bow to this moment: something allowed you to breathe, so figure out why you got to wake up today. Figure out why you got the ability to smile today because someone else didn't. Where can your smile change someone's day?

NAMA-CRAY CALL TO ACTION

2. **What does it take to be seen and fully show up? Vulnerability is the pathway to real love.**

A. Bow to your vulnerabilities: they are the pathway to real connection. It's not going to be easy, but it will be worth it. Where can you let someone in?

B. Bow to your fears: being truly seen in all your f-ugly is the only way out. Who deserves to see all of you today?

NAMA-CRAY CALL TO ACTION

3. **It takes courage to choose faith over fear. A courageous heart knows not to compete with the flow, even if it's not what you asked for.**

A. Bow to faith in your path: it's a way to reach inner contentment in what's given. Get out of your own way. Where are you fighting life?

B. Bow to trust: it's easier to see bad than good, so be

courageous enough to see the good. Don't let it be a boulder in your way; keep going until it feels like a fucking stepping stone. Why not create meaning and move forward?

NAMA-CRAY CALL TO ACTION

4. Who you are in the downfall matters more than who you are on the way back up. The practice of sitting in discomfort is a necessary part of life, so trust the wisdom of uncertainty.

   A. Bow to the breakdown: it creates breakthroughs. Messy is beautiful and sticky and awful and worth it. They didn't say it was going to be easy, but they said it would be worth it. Where can you add trust to a current breakdown?

   B. Bow to the Rock Bottom Café: at least from there, the only way to go is up. Where are you excited to break through and move forward?

NAMA-CRAY CALL TO ACTION

5. Life happens *for* and *from* you. You can't control what happens, but you can control the meaning you give to it.

   A. Bow to the experience: there's a strength that grows from your story. You dictate the meaning. What part of your life can you create meaning around?

   B. Bow to the shitty parts of life: they make good stories. How you tell your story is how the world will remember you. What narrative are you writing about your life?

NAMA-CRAY CALL TO ACTION

6. It's a constant journey of knowing yourself. Your inner GPS is always guiding...if you dare to listen.
   A. Bow to your inner GPS, even when it fucking hurts: it will always guide you if you're willing to hear it. What are you avoiding?
   B. Bow to your inner GPS: it's always guiding, but sometimes, you forget to turn the volume up. Be in service to your self-love—love yourself the way you wanted them to love you. Where can you love yourself more audaciously?

NAMA-CRAY CALL TO ACTION

7. True, lasting happiness is a practice of constant growth. Fall in love with the process of self-inquiry and you'll have a love affair with yourself that never ends.
   A. Bow to your journey of growth: true happiness is the conditioning of discovery and growth. Bow to the lifelong adventure you get to have with the coolest person you know, yourself. Where can you turn your lens of focus to growth?
   B. Bow to your inner cray: that's what makes the jour-

ney so damn interesting. True self-worth can only be quantified through your own description of success.

NAMA-CRAY CALL TO ACTION

8. **Bow to the New You and Fuck the Q. Balance isn't found; it's created.**

   A. Bow to the shedding of old ways: the only way through is forward, and it doesn't matter who comes with you. Where can you just take one step today that makes you proud?

   B. Bow to the work: the messy, gooey, hard work. Luck is the residue of your design. You're in the driver's seat, so where can you take back control?

About the Author

KATIE B. HAPPYY has always taken inner transformation seriously. The fire in Katie B.'s spirit took a giant pause when she woke up in 2015 with Bell's palsy and the right side of her face paralyzed. Katie B. used her paralysis to give up definitions of societal normal beauty and aims to create not just work *outs*, but work *ins*. From her BA in international conflict resolution to her over 10,000 hours of master yoga/fitness certifications, her global company has changed thousands of lives. **b inspired, LLC, & charity organization** helps you rediscover your power. From life-changing Self-Venture International Retreats to epic online Zoom classes, the b_inspired team helps you align up to your clarity in your calling.

Katie has appeared on NBC and CBS, been featured in *Shape* magazine, and serves as an international lululemon model/ambassador. She has taught at many festivals, including Wanderlust; been a presenter at the International Yoga Festival in Rishikesh, India; and created her own bi-coastal "Sweat for Service" event where hundreds give back to the families of fallen soldiers. The tragic loss of her young, forty-three-year-old mom from breast cancer helped fuel Katie to create her 501(c)3, b_inspired, which helps people discover who they are after loss. She's taken hundreds of cancer survivors on healing weekends to start fresh and redefine their power. To nominate someone, visit www.binspired.life.

Through her b_inspired courses, which have been hosted in over thirty countries, and her massively inspirational www. youtube.com/katiebhappyy, Katie B. challenges thousands to awaken a deeper part of their spirit.